Martha White
SOUTHERN BAKING BOOK

A Benjamin **b** Company Book

Project Coordinators:	Jim King, Linda Thompson
Chief Home Economist:	Betty Sullivan
Food Technician:	Roberta Pressman
Recipe Consultant:	Ernestine Minnitt
Editor:	Julie Hogan
Editorial Assistants:	Susan A. Jablonski, Virginia Schomp, Greta Ebel, Janelle Steybe, Tenna Faler, Beth Politi
Art & Design:	Thomas C. Brecklin
Typography:	A-Line, Milwaukee
Food Stylist:	Carol Peterson
Propping:	Toni D'Orr
Photography:	Teri Sandison, Los Angeles

Merchandise courtesy Bullock's Home Store, Bullock's
Beverly Center, Los Angeles

Martha White Foods, Inc.
P.O. Box 58
Nashville, TN 37202

Prepared and published by: The Benjamin Company, Inc.
One Westchester Plaza
Elmsford, NY 10523

ISBN: 0-87502-117-4
Library of Congress Catalog Card Number: 82-073918

9 8 7 6 5 4 3 2 1

TABLE OF CONTENTS

Welcome . . .

to the **Martha White Southern Baking Book.** Our first complete cookbook just had to be a collection of the most-requested recipes from the Martha White Kitchens. However, we've also included a chapter on the basics of baking and some new recipes we hope you will enjoy.

Many of you have been our friends for years. We know that you depend on Martha White flour, corn meal, and convenience mixes and we are always working to maintain the confidence you have in us.

Of course, this book would not be complete without a special tribute to Alice Jarman who was the Director of the Martha White Kitchens for 28 years. Alice started a tradition here for developing good, basic recipes using ingredients that you usually have right there in your kitchen. These are the kinds of recipes that have become Southern classics.

Please feel free to write me if you have questions concerning any of our recipes or products. We'll help all we can. Now, enjoy the **Martha White Southern Baking Book.** I hope it will become a trusted friend in your kitchen.

Warmest regards,

Linda Thompson
Director
Martha White Kitchens

The Martha White Story

It all started in 1899 when the owner of the Royal Flour Mill in Nashville, Tennessee named his favorite flour for his three-year-old daughter, Martha White Lindsey. That's where Martha White Foods, Inc. got its name, and today the picture of that same little girl appears on every package of more than 125 Martha White products.

Established in the Southeast as a leading producer of flour, corn meal, and convenience mix products, Martha White Foods is recognized as a hallmark of quality, innovation, and tradition — particularly in Southern-style bread baking.

Cooks know to "trust Martha White for all their baking." Martha White products are kitchen-tested to meet high standards of taste and performance.

As an innovator, Martha White pioneered the development of self-rising flour and corn meal. The now-famous Hot Rize® put the salt and baking powder right in the mix, creating a forerunner of modern ready-to-bake convenience mixes.

Martha White's serving-size BixMix® packages spurred the industry's direction toward convenience mix packaging. This was actually a reflection of the days when flour was only available by the barrel. Then Royal Flour Mill started something new by repackaging flour in nickel and dime quantities to appeal to customers who could better afford that amount.

Tradition at Martha White has been built on stories like that and by the company's long-time involvement with country music. Martha White's relationship with the legendary Grand Ole Opry is renowned. The company's early-morning sponsorship on WSM radio led to the discovery of the world's most famous bluegrass music group: Lester Flatt, Earl Scruggs, and the Foggy Mountain Boys. That relationship spawned the Martha White theme song — now a bluegrass standard.

During an appearance at Carnegie Hall, Lester Flatt and Earl Scruggs were surprised and delighted to hear requests shouted from the audience for the famous Martha White jingle. They complied, and their banjos rang out with:

> *"Now you bake right (Ah ha) —*
> *With Martha White (yes, ma'am) —*
> *Goodness Gracious, Good and Light,*
> *Martha White.*
>
> *For the finest biscuits, cakes, and pies —*
> *Martha White Self-Rising Flour,*
> *The one all-purpose flour*
> *Martha White Self-Rising Flour has got Hot Rize."*

It's all a part of the Martha White story. From one little girl in 1899 to the kitchens of America, Martha White is a warm blend of yesterday's traditions, today's technology, and tomorrow's new products.

The Basics of Baking

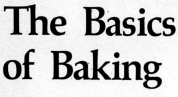

How is yeast dissolved? What kind of pan should bread be baked in? How long should cake cool in the pan? These are only a few of the many questions that are answered in this chapter. The Basics of Baking is designed to give both new and seasoned cooks a broad basis of baking information that will help them create the very best breads, coffeecakes, biscuits, cakes, and pies.

ABOUT BAKING WITH YEAST

Yeast is a leavening agent that acts with sugar in the dough to form carbon dioxide gas. It is this action which causes the dough to rise and gives the finished bread lightness. There are two forms of yeast: compressed cakes (in .6 ounce packages) and active dry yeast (in 1/4 ounce packages and 4 ounce jars). They can be used interchangeably. One package dry yeast equals 2 2/3 teaspoons or one .6 ounce cake.

Flour Facts

Wheat flour, either white or whole wheat, is the flour most commonly used to make bread because it contains gluten, a substance that causes the dough to expand into an elastic framework that holds the gas formed by the yeast. Because whole wheat flour contains less gluten, it is usually used in combination with white. Other flours can be used to make bread, but only in combination with white flour. The recipes in this book have been specially formulated using Martha White All-Purpose, Self-Rising, and Whole Wheat Flours. When using the all-purpose and whole wheat flours to make bread, it is not necessary to sift the flour before measuring. Simply spoon flour lightly into a measuring cup, and level with a knife. Self-Rising flour may be substituted in any yeast bread recipe by omitting the salt from the recipe ingredients. Because heat and humidity can affect the amount of flour needed for a given recipe, you might have to add up to 1 cup more flour on a hot, humid day. Store flour in airtight containers, ideally in the refrigerator or freezer.

Other Ingredients

Water, potato cooking water, and milk (whole, skim, reconstituted dry, evaporated, or buttermilk) are the liquids most often used in bread making. Modern day pasteurization of milk has enabled us to do away with scalding milk prior to using it. If, however, you are using fresh, unpasteurized milk, scald and cool before using. When using active dry yeast, the temperature of the liquid should be between 105°F and 115°F if dissolving the yeast directly in water, or 120°F to 130°F if combining the yeast and flour prior to adding the liquid. When using compressed yeast cakes, the liquid should be between 80°F and 90°F. Never use liquids that are too hot because the yeast will be killed and the dough will not rise.

The addition of sugar to bread dough is necessary to produce the gas which makes the dough rise. Sugar also adds flavor and aids browning. The most commonly used sugars are granulated, brown, molasses, and honey. Salt is added not only for flavor but to also inhibit the action of the yeast, actually controlling the rising time. Fats (margarine, butter, lard, vegetable shortening, and oils) tenderize the bread, giving it a tender, soft crumb. Eggs add flavor, nutrition, and richness. They also produce a fine crumb and tender crust. The addition of fruits, nuts, herbs, spices, or cheese provides variety, flavor, and nutrition. Use sparingly, because these additional ingredients slow rising time.

BREAD MAKING TERMS

These commonly used bread making terms are explained to help you short-cut your way through any recipe.

Kneading

This is the process that completes mixing through rhythmic pressure on the dough. Kneading should be done on a lightly floured board or pastry cloth. First, rub a little flour on your hands to keep the dough from sticking. Shape the dough into a ball. Fold the dough, bringing it toward you. Push down with the heel of your hand; give the dough a slight turn; fold and press again. Repeat until the dough becomes smooth, elastic, and satiny. This should take 8 to 10 minutes. If the dough is sticky, sprinkle the board or pastry cloth with a little flour. Use firm, steady, but gentle pressure. When kneading is completed, place the dough in a large greased bowl. Turn once to grease the top. Cover bowl with waxed paper, plastic wrap, or damp cloth.

Rising

Rising is the process of letting the dough double in bulk, at least once, and often twice. Rising of yeast breads, except refrigerator doughs, should be done in a warm place (80°F to 85°F), free from draft. An excellent place for dough to rise is in the oven. Place the bowl in a cold oven with a pan of hot water. Dough has risen sufficiently when it is double in bulk. To check for doubling, press two fingertips lightly about 1/2 inch into the dough. If a dent remains after you withdraw your fingers, the dough has risen sufficiently.

Punch Down

After the dough has risen, it must be punched down to expel air and redistribute the yeast. Push fist firmly into the center of the dough; bring edge toward center and turn dough over.

Let Rest

This step, after kneading but before shaping, makes dough easier to handle. Usually ten minutes are allowed. If you are short of time, this step can be omitted.

Shaping

For recipes yielding 2 loaves, divide the dough in half. Roll out each half with a rolling pin or pat into a 14 × 9-inch rectangle (for an 8 1/2 × 4 1/2 × 2 1/2-inch pan) or 15 × 10 inches (for a 9 × 5 × 3-

Form dough into a ball for kneading.

The two-fingertip test for doubling.

Punch down dough when double in bulk.

Shape loaf by rolling up dough.

inch pan). Roll up the rectangles tightly from the narrow side, pressing with your thumbs to seal the dough at each turn. Pinch the edges and ends to seal. Fold the ends under. Place the loaf in the pan with both ends touching the pan. Brush the top of the loaf with melted butter or vegetable oil. Cover and place in a warm place, free from draft, until double in bulk.

BAKING AND STORING

Preheat

The proper preheated temperature provides the "oven spring" which is the final expansion of the dough. If using glass pans, reduce oven temperature by 25°F.

Pan Placement

Place pans 2 inches apart on the middle shelf of the oven. Four pans should be staggered on 2 shelves. Avoid placing pans directly above and below each other.

Testing Doneness

When baking time is completed, remove the pan from the oven. Turn the loaf out of the pan. Tap the bottom and sides of the loaf. If the loaf sounds hollow, it is fully baked.

Cooling

Immediately turn bread out onto a wire rack to keep it from becoming soggy as it cools.

Storing

Bread should be cooled completely before wrapping, storing, or freezing. Homemade breads stay fresh and moist when tightly wrapped in aluminum foil, plastic wrap, or an airtight plastic bag, and stored in a cool, dry place.

Thawing

Thaw frozen bread in its wrapper 2 to 3 hours at room temperature. If bread is wrapped in aluminum foil, it can be thawed quickly by placing it in a 375°F oven for 20 minutes. Sweet yeast breads should be thawed before frosting and decorating.

11

SHAPING YEAST ROLLS

Pan Rolls

Gently shape pieces of dough into smooth, 1 1/2-inch balls by pulling the dough down and under with your thumb. Place, smooth sides up, in greased muffin cups or an 8-inch round baking pan about 1/2 inch apart.

Cloverleaf Rolls

Shape pieces of dough into smooth, 3/4-inch balls. Place 3 balls in each greased muffin cup.

Easy Cloverleaf Rolls

Shape dough as for pan rolls. Place 1 ball in each greased muffin cup. Use scissors dipped in flour to cut each ball crosswise in half, then into quarters, cutting almost through to the bottom.

Parker House Rolls

Roll out dough to 1/4-inch thickness on lightly floured board or pastry cloth. Cut out with a floured 2 1/2-inch round cutter. Use the floured handle of a knife to make a deep, off-center crease in the top of each round. Fold the larger section over the smaller section. Press edges together lightly. Place about 1 1/2 inches apart on greased baking sheet.

Fan Tans

Roll out dough into 12 × 9-inch rectangle. Brush with melted butter. Cut lengthwise into 6 strips. Stack the strips. Cut into twelve 1-inch pieces. Place, cut sides up, in greased muffin cups.

Twists

Shape pieces of dough into 1 1/2-inch balls. Roll each ball into a thin, 12-inch rope. Fold in half; twist in center. Pinch ends to seal. Place about 2 inches apart on a greased baking sheet.

Double Knots

Shape pieces of dough into 1 1/2-inch balls. Roll each ball into a thin, 12-inch rope. Form into a loose knot at center, leaving two long ends. Bring the top end under the rope, tucking it into the center of the knot. Bring the bottom end over the rope, tucking it into the center of the knot. Place 2 1/2 inches apart on greased baking sheet.

Double Knots

Cloverleaf Rolls

Easy Cloverleaf Rolls

Parker House Rolls

BISCUIT BASICS AND TECHNIQUES

The delicious biscuit recipes in this book are all made with Martha White Self-Rising Flour. This flour contains baking powder which makes the dough rise and salt which adds flavor. Our recipes require that the flour be sifted to add air to the flour, which helps make the biscuits light. If using Martha White All-Purpose Flour, sift 1 1/2 teaspoons baking powder and scant 1/2 teaspoon salt into every 1 cup all-purpose flour.

13

General Method for Making Biscuits

With a pastry blender or two knives, cut in shortening until mixture is the consistency of coarse crumbs. These bits of shortening make biscuits flaky. Make a well in the dry ingredients. Add liquid all at once. Stir with a fork until the dough leaves the sides of the bowl and forms a ball. Turn the dough out onto a floured board or pastry cloth. Roll the dough around to coat lightly with flour. Knead gently to combine ingredients thoroughly. With a rolling pin, roll evenly to desired thickness, usually about 1/2 inch. Biscuits will double in height during baking. Cut close together with floured biscuit cutter so there is less dough to reroll. Use straight downward motion, not a twisting one. Gently press leftover dough together and reroll. The best utensil for baking biscuits is a shiny, lightly greased baking sheet. For crusty sides, place the biscuits 1 inch apart. For soft sides, place the biscuits close together.

Freezing Biscuits

Although biscuits are best when baked soon after mixing the dough, the dough can be frozen for later use.

To freeze, prepare biscuit dough according to the recipe. Roll out, cut, and place biscuits on a lightly greased baking sheet. Brush the tops lightly with milk. Place in the freezer. When frozen hard (about 1 hour), remove the baking sheet from the freezer. Place biscuits in a plastic bag; seal the bag and return it to freezer.

When ready to use, remove the bag from the freezer and place the biscuits on a lightly greased baking sheet. Preheat oven to 450°F. Biscuits do not have to thaw before baking. Bake 12 to 15 minutes, or until golden brown.

TIPS FOR PERFECT SHORTENING CAKES

To make a moist, velvety shortening-type cake, follow the recipe carefully. And, for best results, do the following:

☐ Sift flour before measuring.

☐ Cream shortening and sugar until light and fluffy, or until sugar is dissolved.

☐ Always use fresh eggs. Eggs separate easily when cold, but should be at room temperature for beating the whites.

- Preheat oven to correct temperature. If using glass pans, reduce oven temperature by 25°F.
- If using melted chocolate, cool slightly before stirring it into batter.
- Scrape sides of bowl frequently with a rubber spatula during mixing.
- Use baking pans with a shiny surface. Grease and lightly flour the pan or grease the bottom and cover it with greased waxed paper.
- Spread batter evenly in pans.
- Position pans as near to center of oven as possible. Pans should not touch sides of oven or each other.
- Cool cake in a layer pan 10 minutes and in a loaf pan 15 minutes before loosening the edge and turning it out onto a wire rack to cool.
- Use vegetable shortening if the recipe calls for it. Do not use a substitute.
- Cool cake completely before frosting, unless the recipe instructs otherwise.
- Cake is done when the sides shrink slightly away from the pan and a cake tester or toothpick inserted in the center comes out clean.

CONVERTING RECIPES TO MICROWAVE OVEN COOKING

Consider using the microwave oven for making many of our recipes. Be sure to use glass or microwave-safe baking pans, and follow these general instructions for baking in the microwave:

To make yeast or quick breads:
- Use a loaf pan 1/2 to 1 inch larger than called for in the recipe. If you do not have a larger pan, remove some of the batter to a smaller container and cook separately.
- Choose yeast bread recipes that have corn meal, bran, whole wheat flour, or rye flour to obtain rich color.
- When preparing yeast dough, use a glass measure and temperature probe set at 120°F to heat liquid and shortening.
- Fill paper-lined muffin cups only half full of batter.
- Coffeecakes and breads bake especially well in a bundt-type pan or ring mold.

15

◻ Quick breads cook quickly, have even texture and greater volume when baked in the microwave oven, but they do not brown. Top with any of the following for a colorful, appealing appearance: toasted coconut, crumbled bacon, cinnamon and sugar, chopped nuts, cheese, sesame seed, crushed cereals, or frosting.

To make microwave cakes or bar cookies:

◻ Enhance light-colored batters with brown sugar, nutmeg, cinnamon, coffee, nuts, icings, or glazes.

◻ Bake layer cakes one layer at a time.

◻ Rotate baking dish a quarter turn if cake is rising unevenly.

◻ Do not attempt angel food or sponge cake in the microwave. They are best baked in a conventional oven.

To make microwave pies:

◻ Use glass pie pans.

◻ Test for doneness of a pastry shell: surface should appear dry and opaque.

SUBSTITUTIONS AND EQUIVALENTS

Flour: 1 cup self-rising flour = 1 cup all-purpose flour plus 1 1/2 teaspoons baking powder and scant 1/2 teaspoon salt. ("All-purpose" flour is the same as "plain" flour.)

Milk: 1 cup whole milk = 1/2 cup evaporated milk plus 1/2 cup water or 1 cup reconstituted nonfat dry milk plus 2 1/2 teaspoons melted butter or margarine.

Buttermilk: 1 cup buttermilk = 1 cup sweet milk plus 1 tablespoon lemon juice or vinegar. Let stand 5 minutes.

Yeast: 1 cake compressed yeast (.6 ounces) = 1 package (1/4 ounce) active dry yeast = 2 2/3 teaspoons active dry yeast.

Chocolate: 1 square (1 ounce) unsweetened baking chocolate = 3 tablespoons cocoa plus 1 tablespoon butter or margarine.

Herbs: 1 tablespoon fresh snipped herbs = 1 teaspoon dried herbs.

Baskets of Biscuits & Muffins

Can you imagine anything more reassuring than a basket of homemade biscuits, kept hot and hidden under a colorful napkin? Hmmm. Whether it's breakfast, brunch, snack, or supper, you just know that meal will be special. Here's a collection of our favorites to start you off.

Hot Rize Biscuits _____ 12 to 14 biscuits

2 cups sifted Martha White
Self-Rising Flour

1/4 cup vegetable shortening
3/4 cup milk

Preheat oven to 450°F. Lightly grease large baking sheet; set aside. Place flour in bowl; cut in shortening with pastry blender or 2 knives until mixture is consistency of coarse crumbs. Add milk; stir with fork just until dough leaves sides of bowl. Turn out onto lightly floured board or pastry cloth. Knead just until smooth. Roll out dough to 1/2-inch thickness. Cut into rounds with floured 2-inch biscuit cutter. Place on prepared baking sheet. Bake 10 to 12 minutes, or until golden brown.

Thimble Biscuits _____ 12 to 14 biscuits

1 recipe Hot Rize
Biscuits (above)

2 to 3 tablespoons jelly
or jam

Preheat oven to 450°F. Lightly grease large baking sheet; set aside. Prepare biscuit dough. Roll out dough on lightly floured board or pastry cloth to 1/4-inch thickness. Cut into rounds with floured 2-inch biscuit cutter. Place half of biscuits on prepared baking sheet. Use a thimble, or other small cutter, to cut a hole in center of each remaining biscuit. Place a biscuit with center removed on top of each whole biscuit. Fill each hole with about 1/2 teaspoon jelly. Bake 10 to 12 minutes, or until golden brown.

Ginger-Date
Bran Muffins _____ 8 muffins

1 egg
1/3 cup milk
1 tablespoon sugar
1/3 cup chopped dates
1 tablespoon slivered
crystallized ginger

1 package (7 ounces)
Martha White Bran
Muffin Mix

Preheat oven to 425°F. Grease 8 muffin cups; set aside. Beat egg in bowl with fork. Add milk and sugar; stir until sugar is dissolved. Add dates, ginger, and muffin mix; stir just until blended. Fill prepared muffin cups two-thirds full. Bake 15 to 18 minutes, or until golden brown. Serve warm.

Hot Rize Biscuits, Thimble Biscuits, Sausage Show-Offs (page 20) →

Sausage Show-Offs _____ 12 biscuits

1 recipe Hot Rize Biscuits   1 pound pork sausage
(page 18)

Preheat oven to 350°F. Prepare biscuit dough. Roll out dough on lightly floured board or pastry cloth into 1/4-inch thick rectangle. Spread sausage over dough almost to edge. Roll up, jelly-roll fashion. Cut into 1/2-inch thick rounds. Place rounds on ungreased baking sheet. Bake 30 minutes, or until golden brown. Serve immediately.

Biscuit Mix _____ 48 to 56 biscuits

8 cups Martha White   1 cup vegetable shortening
Self-Rising Flour

Sift flour into large bowl. Cut in shortening with pastry blender or 2 knives until mixture is consistency of coarse crumbs. Store in airtight container at room temperature. Mix keeps at least 4 months. To use, stir in milk to make a soft dough. (Use 1/3 cup milk for each 1 cup mix.) Preheat oven to 450°F. Roll out dough on lightly floured board or pastry cloth to 1/2-inch thickness. Cut into rounds with floured 2-inch biscuit cutter. Place biscuits on lightly greased baking sheet. Bake 10 to 12 minutes, or until golden brown.

Cajun Biscuits _____ About 24 biscuits

1 package (1/4 ounce) active   1 cup water
dry yeast   2 tablespoons vegetable oil
1/4 cup warm water (105°F to   2 teaspoons sugar
115°F)
3 1/2 cups Martha White
Self-Rising Flour

Grease 2 large baking sheets; set aside. Dissolve yeast in water in bowl. Add remaining ingredients; mix well. Cover and let rise in warm place, free from draft, 45 minutes, or until double in bulk. Stir down. Drop by tablespoonfuls onto prepared baking sheets. Cover and let rise in warm place, free from draft, 40 minutes, or until almost double in bulk. Preheat oven to 425°F. Bake 18 to 20 minutes, or until golden brown. Serve hot.

20

Cheese and Bacon
Biscuits _____ 12 to 14 biscuits

2 cups sifted Martha White
   Self-Rising Flour
1/4 cup vegetable shortening
1 cup (4 ounces) grated sharp
   Cheddar cheese

1/4 cup (4 strips) crumbled
   crisp-cooked bacon
3/4 cup milk

Preheat oven to 450°F. Lightly grease baking sheet; set aside. Place flour in bowl. Cut in shortening with pastry blender or 2 knives until mixture is consistency of coarse crumbs. Stir in cheese and bacon. Add milk; stir with fork just until dough leaves sides of bowl. Turn out onto lightly floured surface or pastry cloth. Knead until smooth. Roll out to 1/2-inch thickness. Cut into rounds with floured 2-inch biscuit cutter. Place on prepared baking sheet. Bake 10 to 12 minutes, or until golden brown.

In a Nashville appearance, comedian Bob Hope once told the Opry House audience: "This Grand Ole Opry gives you a feeling of power. When you step on the floor, your spirits soar, like Martha White Self-Rising Flour."

Old-Fashioned
Buttermilk Biscuits _____ 12 to 14 biscuits

2 cups sifted Martha White
   Self-Rising Flour
1/4 teaspoon baking soda

1/4 cup vegetable shortening
7/8 cup buttermilk

Preheat oven to 450°F. Lightly grease baking sheet; set aside. Combine flour and baking soda in bowl. Cut in shortening with pastry blender or 2 knives until mixture is consistency of coarse crumbs. Add buttermilk; stir with fork just until dough leaves sides of bowl. Turn out onto lightly floured board or pastry cloth. Knead gently just until smooth. Roll out to 1/2-inch thickness. Cut into rounds with floured 2-inch biscuit cutter. Place on prepared baking sheet. Bake 10 to 12 minutes, or until golden brown.

Applesauce Muffins _____ 12 muffins

2 cups sifted Martha White
   Self-Rising Flour
1/3 cup sugar
1/4 teaspoon nutmeg
1/4 teaspoon cinnamon
1 egg

1 cup applesauce
1/2 cup milk
3 tablespoons vegetable
   shortening, melted, or
   vegetable oil

Preheat oven to 425°F. Grease 12 muffin cups; set aside. Sift flour, sugar, and spices into bowl; set aside. Break egg into separate bowl; beat lightly with fork. Add applesauce, milk, and shortening. Add flour mixture; stir just until blended. Fill muffin cups about three-fourths full. Bake 20 minutes, or until golden brown.

For Banana Muffins, substitute 1 cup mashed bananas for applesauce.

Basic Muffins _____ 12 muffins

1 egg
1 cup milk
3 tablespoons vegetable
   shortening, melted, or
   vegetable oil

2 cups sifted Martha White
   Self-Rising Flour
2 tablespoons sugar

Preheat oven to 425°F. Grease 12 muffin cups; set aside. Break egg into bowl; beat lightly with fork. Stir in milk and shortening. Add flour and sugar; stir just until blended. Fill muffin cups about two-thirds full. Bake 20 minutes, or until golden brown.

For Blueberry Muffins, add 1 cup fresh or frozen blueberries to batter.

← Applesauce Muffins, Basic Muffins (variation)

Date-Nut Muffins _____ 12 muffins

1/2 cup sugar
1/2 cup butter or margarine
1 egg
2 cups sifted Martha White
   Self-Rising Flour

1 cup milk
1 cup chopped dates
1/2 cup chopped nuts

Preheat oven to 375°F. Grease 12 muffin cups; set aside. Cream sugar and butter with electric mixer in mixing bowl until fluffy. Add egg; blend thoroughly. Add flour and milk alternately, beating well after each addition. Fold in dates and nuts. Fill muffin cups about two-thirds full. Bake 20 minutes, or until golden brown.

Pecans, walnuts, filberts, almonds — any nuts will do. Mix them, or choose your favorite!

Easy Cheesy Muffins _____ 12 muffins

1 cup sifted Martha White
   Self-Rising Flour
1 cup Martha White
   Self-Rising Corn Meal
1/4 cup sugar
2/3 cup grated sharp Cheddar
   cheese

1 egg
1 cup milk
2 tablespoons vegetable
   shortening, melted, or
   vegetable oil

Preheat oven to 325°F. Grease 12 muffin cups; set aside. Combine dry ingredients and cheese in bowl. Break egg into separate bowl; beat lightly with fork. Stir in milk and shortening. Add to flour-cheese mixture; blend thoroughly. Fill muffin cups about two-thirds full. Bake 20 minutes, or until golden brown.

In 1941, Martha White brought its message into Nashville homes when it sponsored a 5:45 A.M. radio program called "Martha White Biscuit and Cornbread Time."

English Bran Muffins ———— 12 muffins

1 cup wheat bran cereal
2/3 cup milk
1 egg
1/4 cup vegetable oil

1 cup sifted Martha White
   Self-Rising Flour
1/4 cup sugar

Preheat oven to 400°F. Grease 12 muffin cups; set aside. Combine cereal and milk in bowl; let stand until liquid is absorbed. Add egg and oil; mix well with fork. Sift flour and sugar into egg mixture; stir just until blended. Fill muffin cups two-thirds full. Bake 25 minutes, or until golden brown.

If using Martha White All-Purpose Flour, add 2 1/2 teaspoons baking powder and 1/2 teaspoon salt.

Easy Sweet Rolls ———— 16 to 18 rolls

1 recipe Hot Rize Biscuits
   (page 18)
1/4 cup butter or margarine,
   melted

1/2 cup sugar
1 teaspoon cinnamon
Confectioners Icing
   (page 44)

Preheat oven to 425°F. Prepare biscuit dough. Grease 9-inch round baking pan; set aside. Roll out dough on lightly floured board or pastry cloth into 1/4-inch thick rectangle. Brush top with butter. Combine sugar and cinnamon; sprinkle evenly over dough. Roll up jelly-roll fashion from long side. Cut into 1/2-inch thick rounds. Place rounds, with sides touching, in prepared pan. Bake 18 to 20 minutes, or until golden brown. Remove from oven. Drizzle Confectioners Icing over rolls in pan. Serve warm.

Rolls can also be baked in greased muffin cups at 425°F 12 to 15 minutes.

Sausage Roll-Ups _____ 36 snack rolls

12 sausage links
2 cups sifted Martha White
   Self-Rising Flour
1/4 cup vegetable shortening
1 cup (4 ounces) grated
   Cheddar cheese

1/2 teaspoon dry mustard
Dash cayenne
3/4 cup milk

Brown sausages in skillet over moderate heat; drain and set aside. Preheat oven to 450°F. Lightly grease large baking sheet; set aside. Place flour in bowl; cut in shortening with pastry blender or 2 knives until mixture is consistency of coarse crumbs. Stir in cheese, mustard, and cayenne. Add milk; stir with fork just until dough leaves sides of bowl. Turn out onto lightly floured surface or pastry cloth. Knead until smooth. Roll out to 1/4-inch thickness. Use sharp knife or pizza cutter to cut dough into twelve 3-inch squares. Place 1 sausage link along one side of each square. Roll up; pinch edge of dough to seal. Cut each roll into 3 pieces. Place, seam side down, on prepared baking sheet. Bake 10 to 12 minutes, or until golden brown. Serve hot.

BixMix Bran Muffins _____ 12 muffins

1 egg
1 package (5 1/2 ounces)
   Martha White BixMix
   (1 1/3 cups)
1 cup wheat bran cereal

1/3 cup sugar
1/4 cup raisins
2/3 cup water
1/4 teaspoon vanilla

Preheat oven to 400°F. Generously grease 12 muffin cups; set aside. Beat egg in bowl with fork. Add remaining ingredients; stir just until blended. Batter will be lumpy. Fill prepared muffin cups half full. Bake 20 minutes, or until golden brown.

Let's Loaf
a Little

We've taken to calling them breads or quick breads, but these lovely loaves have an identity crisis. They're so good that they want to be called desserts! Apricot, Strawberry, Toasted Coconut, Banana Nut — it's no wonder. So, let your family decide while you relax and accept the praise.

Quick Cheese Bread _____ 1 loaf

2 packages (5 1/2 ounces each) Martha White BixMix (2 2/3 cups)	1 1/2 cups (6 ounces) grated sharp Cheddar cheese, divided
3/4 cup milk or water	2 tablespoons butter or margarine
2 eggs, lightly beaten	
2 teaspoons dry mustard	

Preheat oven to 350°F. Grease bottom of 9 × 5 × 3-inch loaf pan; set aside. Pour baking mix into bowl. Add milk; mix with wooden spoon until smooth. Add eggs, mustard, and 1 cup cheese; blend well. Pour batter into prepared pan. Sprinkle with remaining 1/2 cup cheese. Dot with butter. Bake 40 to 50 minutes, or until toothpick inserted in center comes out clean. Cool in pan 10 minutes. Gently loosen sides of loaf. Turn out onto wire rack to cool completely.

Quick Cheese Bread is especially nice as a snack served with raw vegetables. Cut into strips and toast lightly under broiler or in toaster oven.

You may prefer to make this in a somewhat smaller glass loaf pan than specified. It rises a bit higher and is more attractive, for example, in an 8½ × 4½ × 2½-inch pan.

Martha White's strong leadership in 4-H activities began in 1950. Alice Jarman, past test kitchen director and home economist, always enjoyed working with the 4-H'ers and relates this story about her efforts to encourage the youngsters to bake cakes instead of biscuits. "I couldn't understand why they (the children) didn't want to bake cakes," she said, "until I found out that this particular group rode to the contest in school buses, and they figured it was tough enough riding the bus, without squashing their biscuits."

Quick Cheese Bread →

Toasted Coconut Bread _____ 1 loaf

1 1/3 cups shredded coconut	1 egg, lightly beaten
3 cups sifted Martha White Self-Rising Flour	1 1/3 cups milk
1 cup sugar	1 teaspoon vanilla
1 tablespoon grated orange peel	Almond Butter Spread (page 34)

Preheat oven to 350°F. Spread coconut in shallow baking pan. Bake 7 to 12 minutes, or until lightly browned, stirring or shaking pan often to toast coconut evenly; set aside. Grease bottom of 9 × 5 × 3-inch loaf pan; set aside. Sift flour and sugar into bowl. Stir in toasted coconut and orange peel. Combine egg, milk, and vanilla in separate bowl; mix lightly. Combine milk mixture with flour mixture; mix just until blended; do not beat. Pour into prepared pan. Bake 55 to 60 minutes, or until toothpick inserted in center comes out clean. Cool in pan 10 minutes. Loosen sides of loaf. Turn out onto wire rack to cool completely. Cut into thin slices and serve with Almond Butter Spread.

Apricot Bread _____ 1 loaf

2 3/4 cups sifted Martha White Self-Rising Flour	3 tablespoons butter or margarine, melted
3/4 cup sugar	1 1/2 cups uncooked dried apricots, cut into strips
1/4 teaspoon baking soda	
1 cup buttermilk	
1 egg, lightly beaten	1/2 cup chopped pecans

Preheat oven to 350°F. Grease bottom of 9 × 5 × 3-inch loaf pan; set aside. Sift flour, sugar, and baking soda into bowl. Combine buttermilk, egg, and butter in separate bowl. Combine buttermilk mixture and flour mixture; mix just until blended. Stir in apricots and pecans. Pour into prepared pan. Bake 55 to 60 minutes, or until toothpick inserted in center comes out clean. Cool in pan 10 minutes. Gently loosen sides of loaf. Turn out onto wire rack to cool completely.

For delicious party sandwiches, serve thin slices of Apricot Bread spread with softened cream cheese or any of the spreads on page 36.

Prune-Nut Bread _____ 1 loaf

1 cup chopped prunes	3/4 cup sugar
1/2 teaspoon grated orange peel	1/2 teaspoon cinnamon
1/2 cup orange juice	1 tablespoon vegetable shortening, melted, or vegetable oil
1/2 cup hot water	
2 cups sifted Martha White Self-Rising Flour	2 eggs, lightly beaten
	1/2 cup chopped nuts

Combine prunes and orange peel in small bowl. Stir in orange juice and water; let stand 10 minutes. Preheat oven to 350°F. Grease bottom of 9 × 5 × 3-inch loaf pan; set aside. Combine flour, sugar, and cinnamon in bowl; set aside. Add shortening and eggs to prune mixture; stir to blend. Add to flour mixture; blend thoroughly. Stir in nuts. Pour into prepared pan. Bake 50 to 55 minutes, or until toothpick inserted in center comes out clean. Cool in pan 10 minutes. Gently loosen sides of loaf. Turn out onto wire rack to cool completely.

The smaller 8½ × 4½ × 2½-inch glass loaf pan works well for this loaf.

Blueberry Sour Cream Loaf _____ 1 loaf

2 eggs	2 packages (7 ounces each) Martha White Blueberry Muffin Mix
1 cup (8 ounces) dairy sour cream	
1/2 cup milk	1/2 cup chopped pecans
2 tablespoons butter or margarine, melted	

Preheat oven to 350°F. Grease bottom of 9 × 5 × 3-inch loaf pan; set aside. Break eggs into bowl and beat lightly. Add sour cream, milk, butter, and muffin mix; stir just until blended. Stir in pecans. Pour into prepared pan. Bake 45 to 50 minutes, or until toothpick inserted in center comes out clean. Cool in pan 10 minutes. Gently loosen sides of loaf. Turn out onto wire rack to cool completely.

For Apple Cinnamon Sour Cream Loaf, substitute Apple Cinnamon Muffin Mix for Blueberry Muffin Mix.

Festive Pumpkin Bread _____ 1 loaf

1 2/3 cups sifted Martha White
    Self-Rising Flour
1 1/4 cups sugar
    1/2 teaspoon cinnamon
    1/2 teaspoon nutmeg
    2 eggs

1 cup canned pumpkin
1/2 cup vegetable oil
1/3 cup water
1/2 cup candied red cherries,
    chopped
1/2 cup chopped nuts

Preheat oven to 350°F. Grease bottom of 9 × 5 × 3-inch loaf pan; set aside. Sift flour, sugar, cinnamon, and nutmeg into large bowl; set aside. Break eggs into separate bowl and beat lightly. Add pumpkin, oil, and water; blend well. Gradually stir in flour mixture; beat until smooth. Stir in cherries and nuts. Pour into prepared pan. Bake 55 to 60 minutes, or until toothpick inserted in center comes out clean. Cool in pan 10 minutes. Gently loosen sides of loaf. Turn out onto wire rack to cool completely.

For plain Pumpkin Bread, omit cherries and nuts.

Sour Cream
Coffee Loaf _____ 1 loaf

1/2 cup chopped nuts
3 tablespoons brown sugar
1 teaspoon cinnamon
1/2 cup butter or margarine
1 1/4 cups sugar
3 eggs

1 cup (8 ounces) dairy
    sour cream
1 teaspoon grated lemon peel
2 cups sifted Martha White
    Self-Rising Flour

Preheat oven to 350°F. Grease bottom of 9 × 5 × 3-inch loaf pan; set aside. Combine nuts, brown sugar, and cinnamon in small bowl; set aside. Cream sugar and butter with electric mixer in mixing bowl until light and fluffy. Add eggs, 1 at a time, beating well after each addition. Stir in sour cream and lemon peel. Gradually add flour, mixing just until blended. Pour half of the batter into prepared pan. Spoon half of the nut mixture over batter. Spoon on remaining batter. Sprinkle with remaining nut mixture; press nuts gently into top. Bake 50 to 60 minutes, or until golden brown. Cool in pan 10 minutes. Gently loosen sides of loaf. Turn out onto wire rack to cool completely.

Pecans are nice with this loaf but any nuts of your choice may be used.

Strawberry Bread ———————————— 1 loaf

1/2 cup sugar	1/2 teaspoon salt
1/2 cup butter or margarine	1/4 teaspoon baking soda
1 teaspoon vanilla	1 cup strawberry preserves
2 eggs	1/2 cup buttermilk
2 cups sifted Martha White All-Purpose Flour	1/2 cup chopped walnuts

Preheat oven to 325°F. Grease bottom of 9 × 5 × 3-inch loaf pan; set aside. Cream sugar, butter, and vanilla with electric mixer in mixing bowl until light and fluffy. Add eggs, 1 at a time, beating well after each addition. Sift flour, salt, and baking soda into separate bowl; set aside. Combine preserves and buttermilk in small bowl; blend thoroughly. Alternately add flour mixture and preserves mixture to creamed mixture; beat just until blended. Stir in walnuts. Pour into prepared pan. Bake 1 hour 30 minutes, or until toothpick inserted in center comes out clean. Cool in pan 10 minutes. Gently loosen sides of loaf. Turn out onto wire rack to cool completely.

For an especially attractive loaf, try a 8½ × 4½ × 2½-inch glass loaf pan.

Steamed Brown Bread ——————— 2 loaves

1 cup Martha White Self-Rising Corn Meal	3/4 cup molasses
1 cup Martha White Self-Rising Flour	1 teaspoon baking soda
	2 cups buttermilk
1 cup Martha White Whole Wheat Flour	1 cup seedless raisins

Grease two 1-pound cans; set aside. Combine corn meal, flours, and molasses in bowl. Stir baking soda into buttermilk; add to flour mixture; blend thoroughly. Stir in raisins. Pour half of the batter into each prepared can. Cover tops of cans with aluminum foil; secure with string. Place a rack in a pan large enough to hold both cans. Place cans on rack. Add enough water to come halfway up sides of cans. Cover and bring water to a boil. Reduce heat; cook over very low heat 3 hours, adding more water if necessary. Remove cans from pan. Gently loosen sides of bread. Turn out of cans. Slice and serve warm.

To keep bread from crumbling when it's cut, use a piece of heavy string to pull across bread in a sawing motion, or use an electric knife.

Lemon Tea Bread ———————— 1 loaf

3/4 cup sugar
1/3 cup butter or margarine
2 eggs, lightly beaten
3 teaspoons grated lemon
  peel
2 cups sifted Martha White
  Self-Rising Flour

3/4 cup milk
1/2 cup chopped walnuts
2 tablespoons sugar
1 tablespoon lemon juice

Preheat oven to 350°F. Grease bottom of 9 × 5 × 3-inch loaf pan; set aside. Cream 3/4 cup sugar and butter with electric mixer in mixing bowl until light and fluffy. Add eggs and lemon peel; blend thoroughly. Alternately add flour and milk to creamed mixture, beginning and ending with flour. Stir in walnuts. Pour into prepared pan. Bake 55 to 60 minutes, or until toothpick inserted in center comes out clean. Combine 2 tablespoons sugar and lemon juice in small dish. Remove bread from oven. Spoon lemon juice mixture evenly over hot bread. Cool in pan 10 minutes. Gently loosen sides of loaf. Turn out onto wire rack to cool completely.

This recipe works well in an 8½ × 4½ × 2½-inch glass loaf pan.

Orange Butter Spread

1/2 cup butter or margarine,
  softened
1 tablespoon orange juice

1 tablespoon grated
  orange peel

Combine all ingredients in small bowl; blend thoroughly.

Almond Butter Spread

1/2 cup butter or margarine,
  softened
1 tablespoon finely chopped
  almonds

1/2 teaspoon almond extract

Combine all ingredients in small bowl; blend thoroughly.

Lemon Tea Bread, Orange Butter Spread, Almond Butter Spread, →
Honey Cream Spread (page 36), Orange Cream Spread (page 36)

Fruit Cream Spread

1 package (3 ounces) cream
   cheese, at room
   temperature

2 tablespoons jelly, jam,
   preserves, or drained
   crushed pineapple

Combine all ingredients in small bowl; blend thoroughly.

Honey Cream Spread

1 package (3 ounces) cream
   cheese, at room
   temperature

1 tablespoon honey
1 teaspoon lemon juice

Combine all ingredients in small bowl; blend thoroughly.

Ginger Cream Spread

1 package (3 ounces) cream
   cheese, at room
   temperature
2 tablespoons finely
   chopped crystallized
   ginger

2 tablespoons finely
   chopped almonds
1 teaspoon milk

Combine all ingredients in small bowl; blend thoroughly.

Devon Cream

1 package (8 ounces) cream
   cheese, at room
   temperature

1/3 cup dairy sour cream
1 tablespoon sugar

Combine all ingredients in small bowl; blend thoroughly.

Orange Cream Spread

1 package (3 ounces) cream
   cheese, at room
   temperature

1 tablespoon orange juice
1 teaspoon grated orange
   peel

Combine all ingredients in small bowl; blend thoroughly.

Try one of these delicious spreads on the Apricot Bread, Apple Bread, Lemon Tea Bread, or Blueberry Sour Cream Loaf.

Apple Bread _____ 1 loaf

1 cup sugar
1/2 cup vegetable shortening
1 teaspoon vanilla
2 eggs
1 tablespoon buttermilk
2 cups sifted Martha White
   Self-Rising Flour

1 teaspoon grated lemon peel
1 1/2 cups chopped peeled
   tart apples
1 tablespoon sugar
1/2 teaspoon cinnamon

Preheat oven to 350°F. Grease bottom of 9 × 5 × 3-inch loaf pan; set aside. Cream 1 cup sugar, shortening, and vanilla with electric mixer in mixing bowl until light and fluffy. Add eggs and buttermilk; blend well. Add flour; blend well. Stir in lemon peel and apples. Pour into prepared pan. Combine 1 tablespoon sugar and cinnamon; sprinkle over batter. Bake 1 hour, or until toothpick inserted in center comes out clean. Cool in pan 10 minutes. Gently loosen sides of loaf. Turn out onto wire rack to cool completely.

Whole Wheat Health Bread _____ 1 loaf

1 cup Martha White
   Whole Wheat Flour
1 cup sifted Martha White
   Self-Rising Flour
1/4 cup sugar
1/2 teaspoon salt
1/4 teaspoon baking soda

1 egg, lightly beaten
1 1/2 cups buttermilk
1/4 cup honey
1/4 cup butter or margarine,
   melted
1/2 cup chopped walnuts
1/2 cup raisins

Preheat oven to 375°F. Grease bottom of 9 × 5 × 3-inch loaf pan; set aside. Combine flours, sugar, salt, and baking soda in large bowl. Combine egg, buttermilk, honey, and butter in separate bowl. Add buttermilk mixture to flour mixture; stir just until moistened. Stir in walnuts and raisins. Pour into prepared pan. Bake 45 to 50 minutes, or until toothpick inserted in center comes out clean. Cool in pan 10 minutes. Gently loosen sides of loaf. Turn out onto wire rack to cool completely.

This loaf does not rise as high as many of the quick breads and will be more compact.

37

Date-Oatmeal Loaf _____ 1 loaf

3/4 cup uncooked quick oats
1 1/4 cups hot milk
1 cup chopped dates
1 egg, lightly beaten
1/4 cup sugar
1/2 cup light or dark corn
  syrup

2 tablespoons butter or
  margarine, melted
2 cups sifted Martha White
  Self-Rising Flour
1/2 teaspoon cinnamon
1/4 teaspoon salt

Combine oats, milk, and dates in bowl; let stand 10 minutes. Preheat oven to 350°F. Grease bottom of 9 × 5 × 3-inch loaf pan; set aside. Add egg, sugar, corn syrup, and butter to milk mixture; blend well. Combine flour, cinnamon, and salt in large bowl. Add milk mixture; stir just until blended. Pour into prepared pan. Bake 50 to 55 minutes, or until toothpick inserted in center comes out clean. Cool in pan 10 minutes. Gently loosen sides of loaf. Turn out onto wire rack to cool completely.

Banana Nut Loaf _____ 1 loaf

2/3 cup sugar
1/3 cup vegetable shortening
2 eggs
1 cup mashed ripe bananas
  (2 to 3)

3 tablespoons buttermilk
2 cups sifted Martha White
  Self-Rising Flour
1/4 teaspoon baking soda
1/2 cup chopped nuts

Preheat oven to 350°F. Grease bottom of 9 × 5 × 3-inch loaf pan; set aside. Cream sugar and shortening with electric mixer in mixing bowl until light and fluffy. Add eggs, bananas, and buttermilk; blend well. Add flour and baking soda; blend well. Stir in nuts. Pour into prepared pan. Bake 50 to 60 minutes, or until toothpick inserted in center comes out clean. Cool in pan 10 minutes. Gently loosen sides of loaf. Turn out onto wire rack to cool completely.

If you would like a more compact, higher loaf, use an 8 1/2 × 4 1/2 × 2 1/2-inch glass loaf pan.

Breakfast, Brunch, or Munch

Can you imagine awakening to the aroma of a homemade coffeecake? Just the thing to bring the family running to the kitchen, ready to meet the day. Or, how about a piled-high platter of doughnuts for an after school treat? Here you'll also find special brunch fare, like our Ham and Swiss Cheese Quiche or Party Sausage Balls — so get on the phone and invite some friends!

Swedish Tea Ring _____ 3 coffeecakes

1 1/2 cups milk	6 1/2 to 7 cups sifted Martha White
1 1/4 cups plus 2 tablespoons	All-Purpose Flour,
butter or margarine,	divided
divided	3 eggs
1 1/2 cups sugar, divided	1/2 teaspoon vanilla
2 packages (1/4 ounce each)	1 tablespoon cinnamon
active dry yeast	1 cup confectioners sugar
1 1/2 teaspoons salt	1 1/2 to 2 tablespoons milk

Grease large bowl; set aside. Heat 1 1/2 cups milk and 1 cup butter in saucepan until very warm (120°F to 130°F; butter need not melt completely). Combine 1/2 cup sugar, yeast, salt, and 2 cups flour in large mixing bowl. Gradually beat in warm milk mixture at low speed of electric mixer until blended. Beat at medium speed 2 minutes. Add eggs, vanilla, and 2 1/2 cups flour; beat 2 minutes. Use wooden spoon to stir in enough remaining flour to make a soft dough. Turn out onto lightly floured board or pastry cloth. Knead 8 to 10 minutes, or until smooth and elastic. Place dough in prepared bowl. Turn once to grease top. Cover and let rise in warm place, free from draft, 1 hour, or until double in bulk. Punch dough down; divide into thirds. Return 2 thirds to bowl; set aside. Grease 3 large baking sheets; set aside. Roll 1 third dough into 20 × 7-inch rectangle on lightly floured board or pastry cloth. Melt 2 tablespoons butter and brush evenly over dough within 1 inch of edges. Combine remaining 1 cup sugar and cinnamon in small dish; blend well. Sprinkle 1/3 cup sugar-cinnamon mixture evenly over dough within 1 inch of edges. Roll up, jelly-roll fashion, from long side; pinch edges to seal. Place roll, seam side down, on prepared baking sheet. Shape into a ring; pinch ends to seal. Use scissors to cut dough at 1-inch intervals around ring, cutting two-thirds through roll with each cut. Gently turn each cut piece of dough on its side, slightly overlapping slices. Repeat with remaining 2 thirds dough. Cover rings and let rise in warm place, free from draft, 45 minutes, or until double in bulk. Preheat oven to 375°F. Bake 20 to 25 minutes, or until golden brown. Transfer to wire racks. Combine confectioners sugar and 1 1/2 to 2 tablespoons milk in small bowl; blend well. Drizzle over rings while warm.

If desired, 1/2 cup seedless raisins and 1/2 cup chopped pecans can be added to a single cinnamon and sugar filling.

Swedish Tea Rings freeze well, thaw and heat quickly.

Coconut Coffeecake _____ 2 coffeecakes

1 recipe Sweet Yeast Dough
   (page 55)
3 cups grated coconut,
   divided
1/2 cup sugar
1/2 cup butter or margarine

1/4 cup honey
2 tablespoons milk
1/4 teaspoon almond extract
   Confectioners Icing
   (page 44)

Prepare Sweet Yeast Dough. While dough is rising, combine 2 1/2 cups coconut, sugar, butter, honey, and milk in saucepan; bring to a boil, stirring constantly. Remove from heat; let stand until cool. Stir in almond extract. When dough is double in bulk, punch down; let rest 10 minutes. Divide dough in half. Roll out each half into 14 × 8-inch rectangle. Spread half of the coconut filling lengthwise down center 3 inches of 1 rectangle. Beginning 2 inches from 1 end on long side of dough and up to the filling, make 6 slits at 2-inch intervals to outside edge of dough. (This will make 7 strips.) Repeat for other side of dough. Beginning on 1 end, overlap 1 strip from each side over filling. Pull end strips down and under, tucking them in. Repeat with remaining dough rectangle. Cover and let rise in warm place, free from draft, 35 minutes, or until almost double in bulk. Preheat oven to 350°F. Bake 30 to 35 minutes, or until golden brown. Frost with Confectioners Icing while still warm. Sprinkle each coffeecake with 1/4 cup remaining coconut.

Cinnamon Twists _____ 12 to 14 twists

1 recipe Hot Rize Biscuits
   (page 18)
1 cup sugar

2 teaspoons cinnamon
1/2 cup butter or margarine,
   melted

Preheat oven to 450°F. Grease large baking sheet; set aside. Prepare biscuit dough. Roll out to 1/4-inch thickness on lightly floured board or pastry cloth. Cut into rounds with floured 2-inch doughnut cutter. Combine sugar and cinnamon in small bowl; set aside. Dip each round in butter, then in sugar-cinnamon mixture. Twist ends in opposite directions. Place twists 1 inch apart on prepared baking sheet. Bake 10 to 12 minutes, or until golden brown.

41

Bake Shop Doughnuts ———— 24 doughnuts

1 recipe Sweet Yeast Dough
  (page 55)
Oil for deep-fat frying
3 cups sifted confectioners
  sugar

1/2 cup hot milk
1 teaspoon vanilla

Prepare Sweet Yeast Dough. After dough has risen, punch down; let rest 10 minutes. Divide dough in half. Roll out 1 half to 1/3-inch thickness on lightly floured board or pastry cloth. Cut with floured doughnut cutter. Repeat for remaining dough. Let rise, uncovered, in warm place, free from draft, 45 minutes, or until double in bulk. Preheat oil to 375°F in deep-fat fryer or large saucepan. Deep fry doughnuts, a few at a time, 3 to 4 minutes, or until golden brown, turning to brown evenly. Drain on paper towels. Combine confectioners sugar, milk, and vanilla in bowl. Dip doughnuts in confectioners sugar mixture. Transfer to wire rack to cool.

Scones with Devon Cream ———— 12 to 16 scones

2 cups sifted Martha White
  Self-Rising Flour
2 tablespoons sugar
1 teaspoon grated orange
  peel

1/4 teaspoon baking soda
1/4 cup butter or margarine
1 egg, lightly beaten
About 1/2 cup buttermilk
Devon Cream (page 36)

Preheat oven to 400°F. Grease two large baking sheets; set aside. Combine flour, sugar, orange peel, and baking soda in bowl. Cut in butter with pastry blender or 2 knives until mixture is consistency of coarse crumbs. Add egg and buttermilk; mix with fork until well blended. Turn out onto lightly floured board or pastry cloth. Knead just until smooth. Divide dough in half. Pat or roll each half into 1/2-inch thick round. Use floured knife to cut each round into 6 or 8 wedges. Place wedges 1 inch apart on prepared baking sheets. Bake 20 minutes, or until golden brown. Serve hot topped with Devon Cream and strawberry jam, if desired.

To reheat cooled scones, preheat oven to 350°F. Place on ungreased baking sheets. Warm in oven 5 minutes.

Bake Shop Doughnuts, Scones with Devon Cream, Cinnamon Twists (page 41) →

Confectioners Icing _____ 1 1/2 cups

3 cups sifted confectioners
    sugar

1/4 cup hot milk
3/4 teaspoon vanilla

Combine all ingredients in mixing bowl. Beat until smooth.

Whole Wheat
Coffeecake _____ 1 coffeecake

1 cup boiling water
1 package (8 ounces) dates,
    chopped
3/4 cup sifted Martha White
    Self-Rising Flour
3/4 cup Martha White
    Whole Wheat Flour
1/2 cup firmly packed brown
    sugar

1/3 cup sugar
1/2 cup butter or margarine,
    softened
2 eggs, lightly beaten
1 1/2 teaspoons vanilla
    Pecan Glaze (below)

Combine water and dates in small bowl; let stand until cool. Preheat oven to 375°F. Grease and flour 9-inch square baking pan; set aside. Combine flours and sugars in bowl. Cut in butter with pastry blender or 2 knives until mixture is consistency of coarse crumbs. Add date mixture, eggs, and vanilla; stir just until blended. Pour into prepared pan. Bake 35 to 40 minutes, or until cake shrinks away slightly from sides of pan. Remove from oven. Pour Pecan Glaze over cake in pan. Cool 10 to 15 minutes before cutting into squares.

If using Martha White All-Purpose Flour, add 1 1/2 teaspoons baking powder and 1 teaspoon salt.

Pecan Glaze

1 1/2 cups confectioners sugar
3 tablespoons milk
1 teaspoon vanilla

1/2 teaspoon almond extract
1/2 cup chopped pecans

Combine all ingredients except pecans in small bowl; stir until smooth. Stir in pecans.

Honey-Pecan Muffins ———— 12 muffins

3 tablespoons brown sugar
2 tablespoons butter or
  margarine, melted
1 tablespoon honey
12 pecan halves
2 cups sifted Martha White
  Self-Rising Flour

1/2 cup sugar
2 teaspoons cinnamon
3/4 cup milk
1/3 cup vegetable oil

Preheat oven to 425°F. Combine brown sugar, butter, and honey in small bowl. Grease 12 muffin cups. Spoon about 1 teaspoon honey mixture into each cup. Place a pecan half in each cup; set aside. Sift flour, sugar, and cinnamon into bowl. Add milk and oil; stir just until blended. Fill prepared muffin cups about two-thirds full. Bake 15 minutes, or until golden brown. Immediately remove muffins from pan and turn upside down onto wire rack. Serve warm.

Blueberry Nut Coffeecake —— 16 servings

2 packages (7 ounces each)
  Martha White Blueberry
  Muffin Mix
1 cup milk

1/2 cup chopped nuts
  (optional)
Crumble Topping (below)

Preheat oven to 375°F. Grease 9-inch square baking pan; set aside. Pour muffin mix into bowl. Add milk and nuts; stir just until blended. Spread evenly in prepared pan. Sprinkle with Crumble Topping. Use a knife to gently swirl topping into batter; do not mix. Bake 30 to 35 minutes, or until golden brown. Cut into squares and serve warm.

Crumble Topping

1/2 cup firmly packed brown
  sugar
2 tablespoons Martha White
  All-Purpose Flour

1 teaspoon cinnamon
2 tablespoons butter or
  margarine

Combine all ingredients in small bowl; mix with pastry blender or two knives until crumbly.

Ham and Swiss Cheese Quiche _____ 6 to 8 servings

Corn Meal Quiche Crust
(below)
1 1/2 cups cubed smoked ham
1 cup (4 ounces) shredded
Swiss cheese
1 cup half-and-half
4 eggs

1 tablespoon prepared
mustard
1 tablespoon minced green
onion
1/4 teaspoon salt
1/8 teaspoon white pepper

Prepare the Corn Meal Quiche Crust. Preheat oven to 350°F. Sprinkle ham and cheese evenly over bottom of crust. Combine half-and-half, eggs, mustard, green onion, salt, and pepper in bowl; blend well. Pour into crust. Bake 45 to 50 minutes, or until center is set and top is golden brown. Let stand 10 minutes. Cut into wedges.

Corn Meal Quiche Crust _____ One 9-inch crust

2/3 cup Martha White
All-Purpose Flour
1/3 cup Martha White
Self-Rising Corn Meal

1/2 teaspoon salt
1/3 cup vegetable shortening
1 1/2 to 2 tablespoons cold water

Combine flour, corn meal, and salt in bowl. Cut in half of the shortening with pastry blender or 2 knives until mixture is consistency of coarse crumbs. Cut in remaining shortening until mixture is consistency of small peas. Gradually sprinkle water over mixture; stir with fork until moist enough to hold together. Shape into ball. Place on lightly floured board or pastry cloth. Flatten with rolling pin. Roll out into circle about 1 inch larger than 9-inch quiche dish or pie pan. Ease into quiche dish. Trim overhang to 1/2 inch. Fold under to make stand-up edge. Flute edge.

← Ham and Swiss Cheese Quiche

Waffles _____ Twelve 4-inch waffles

2 eggs, separated
1 3/4 cups sifted Martha White
   Self-Rising Flour

1 1/4 cups milk
1/2 cup vegetable shortening,
   melted, or vegetable oil

Preheat waffle iron according to manufacturer's directions. Beat egg whites with electric mixer in mixing bowl until stiff but not dry. Beat yolks in separate mixing bowl until blended. Add flour, milk, and shortening to yolks; blend well. Gently fold in whites with rubber spatula until blended. Bake in hot waffle iron.

Tips on making waffles: Do not pour batter into waffle iron until light goes off. Do not lift lid while waffle is steaming. Waffle is done when steaming stops.

Buttermilk Pancakes _____ 10 pancakes

1 1/4 cups sifted Martha White
   Self-Rising Flour
1 tablespoon sugar
1/2 teaspoon baking soda

1 egg
1 1/4 cups buttermilk
3 tablespoons vegetable
   shortening, melted

Sift flour, sugar, and baking soda into bowl; set aside. Break egg into separate bowl; add buttermilk and shortening; blend well. Add buttermilk mixture to flour mixture; stir just until blended; batter will be lumpy. Preheat skillet or griddle over moderate heat until drop of water sizzles when dropped on skillet. Pour batter 1/4 cup at a time into skillet. Cook until full of bubbles; turn and cook other side until golden brown. If batter becomes too thick, stir in a little water.

Party Sausage Balls _____ 60 appetizers

1/2 pound pork sausage, at
   room temperature
1 cup (4 ounces) shredded
   sharp Cheddar cheese

1 package (5 1/2 ounces)
   Martha White BixMix
   (1 1/3 cups)

Preheat oven to 325°F. Combine sausage and cheese in bowl; blend well with hands. Add baking mix; blend well. Roll mixture into marble-sized balls. Place on ungreased baking sheet. Bake 30 minutes, or until sausage is no longer pink. Serve hot or at room temperature.

Caraway Breadsticks _____ 24 breadsticks

1 package (1/4 ounce) active
dry yeast
1 1/4 cups warm water (105°F
to 115°F)
3 1/2 cups sifted Martha White
All-Purpose Flour

3 tablespoons sugar
3 teaspoons caraway seed,
divided
1 1/2 teaspoons salt
1 tablespoon butter

Grease large bowl; set aside. Dissolve yeast in water in bowl. Add flour, sugar, 2 teaspoons caraway seed, salt, and butter; blend well. Turn out onto lightly floured board or pastry cloth. Knead 8 to 10 minutes, or until smooth and elastic. Shape into ball. Place in prepared bowl. Turn once to grease top. Cover and let rise in warm place, free from draft, 1 hour, or until double in bulk. Punch dough down. Grease 2 large baking sheets; set aside. Shape dough into long roll. Cut into 24 pieces. Use palms of hands to roll each piece into 12-inch stick. Place sticks 1 inch apart on prepared baking sheets. Sprinkle lightly with remaining teaspoon caraway seed. Cover and let rise in warm place, free from draft, 1 hour, or until double in bulk. Preheat oven to 400°F. Bake 15 to 20 minutes, or until golden brown. Transfer to wire rack to cool.

Quick Doughnuts _____ 15 doughnuts

Oil for deep-fat frying
2 cups sifted Martha White
Self-Rising Flour
3 tablespoons sugar
1 teaspoon nutmeg

1/3 cup butter or margarine
1 egg
About 1/3 cup milk
1/2 cup confectioners sugar

Preheat oil to 375°F in deep-fat fryer or large saucepan. Combine flour, sugar, and nutmeg in bowl. Cut in butter with pastry blender or 2 knives; set aside. Beat egg in measuring cup; add milk to measure 2/3 cup. Add to flour mixture; stir with fork until blended. Turn out onto lightly floured board or pastry cloth. Knead just until smooth. Roll out to 1/2-inch thickness. Cut out with floured doughnut cutter. Deep fry doughnuts, a few at a time, 3 to 4 minutes, or until golden brown, turning to brown evenly. Drain on paper towels. Place confectioners sugar in paper bag. Shake 2 doughnuts at a time in bag to coat with sugar. Serve warm.

Cheese Crisps _____ 96 crisps

1 cup butter or margarine,
    softened
2 cups (8 ounces) shredded
    sharp Cheddar cheese

2 cups sifted Martha White
    Self-Rising Flour
2 cups crispy rice cereal
1/8 teaspoon cayenne

Preheat oven to 325°F. Combine all ingredients in bowl; blend well. Use floured fingers to shape into balls the size of large grapes. Place on ungreased baking sheets. Press lightly with fork to 1/4-inch thickness. Bake 20 minutes, or until golden brown. Transfer to wire racks to cool. Store in airtight container.

Corn Cheese Wafers _____ 60 wafers

1 cup sifted Martha White
    Self-Rising Flour
1/2 cup Martha White
    Self-Rising Corn Meal

1/3 cup grated Parmesan cheese
1/2 cup butter or margarine
1/3 cup buttermilk
Poppy or sesame seed

Preheat oven to 350°F. Combine flour, corn meal, and cheese in bowl. Cut in butter with pastry blender or 2 knives until mixture is consistency of coarse crumbs. Add buttermilk; stir just until moistened. Turn out onto lightly floured board or pastry cloth. Knead 4 or 5 times. Roll out to 1/8-inch thickness. Use sharp knife to cut into 3 × 1-inch rectangles. Place on ungreased baking sheets. Prick well with fork. Sprinkle with poppy seed. Bake 10 to 12 minutes, or until golden brown. Transfer to wire racks to cool. Store in airtight container.

Swedish Flatbread _____ 12 crackers

2 1/4 cups sifted Martha White
    Whole Wheat Flour,
    divided
1 cup buttermilk

1 teaspoon salt
1 teaspoon baking soda
1/4 cup butter or margarine,
    melted

Preheat oven to 350°F. Grease large baking sheet; set aside. Combine 1 1/2 cups flour, buttermilk, salt, baking soda, and butter in bowl; stir until smooth. Gradually stir in enough remaining flour to make a stiff dough. Turn out onto floured board or pastry cloth. Knead 3 or 4 times. Divide into 12 portions. Roll each portion into 8-inch circle. Ease dough circles around rolling pin. Lift onto prepared baking sheet. Prick well with fork. Bake 15 minutes, or until lightly browned. Transfer to wire rack to cool. Store in airtight container.

This Dough Will Rise Again

If you have stayed away from yeast baking because you thought it was too hard, or you just couldn't be bothered, this chapter might change your mind. From the basics to specials like Anadama Bread or Hot Cheese Rolls, you'll find that the simplest meals become a feast with your own breads hot from the oven.

Homemade White Bread _____ 2 loaves

1 package (1/4 ounce) active
  dry yeast
1/4 cup warm water (105°F
  to 115°F)
2 cups warm milk
3 tablespoons sugar
1 tablespoon salt

3 tablespoons vegetable
  shortening, melted
5 to 5 1/2 cups Martha White
  All-Purpose Flour,
  divided
Vegetable oil

Dissolve yeast in water in measuring cup. Grease large bowl; set aside. Combine milk, sugar, salt, shortening, and yeast mixture in separate bowl. Add 2 cups flour; blend well. Stir in enough remaining flour to make a stiff dough. Turn out onto floured board or pastry cloth. Cover with bowl. Let rest 10 minutes. Knead dough 8 to 10 minutes, or until smooth and elastic. Shape into ball. Place in prepared bowl. Turn once to grease top. Cover and let rise in warm place, free from draft, 1 1/2 hours, or until double in bulk. Punch down. Let rest 10 minutes. Grease two 9 × 5 × 3-inch loaf pans. Divide dough in half. Shape each half into a loaf. Place in prepared pans. Brush tops with oil. Cover and let rise in warm place, free from draft, 1 hour, or until double in bulk. Preheat oven to 400°F. Bake 15 minutes. Reduce oven temperature to 300°F. Bake 20 to 25 minutes, or until loaves sound hollow when lightly tapped. Transfer to wire rack to cool.

Swedish Limpa Bread _____ 2 loaves

1 cup milk
1 cup water
1/4 cup vegetable shortening
4 cups Martha White
  All-Purpose Flour,
  divided
2 packages (1/4 ounce each)
  active dry yeast

1/4 cup firmly packed brown
  sugar
2 teaspoons caraway seed
1 1/2 cups rye flour
1 tablespoon butter or
  margarine, melted and
  slightly cooled

Grease large bowl; set aside. Heat milk, water and shortening in saucepan until very warm (120°F to 130°F). Combine 3 cups all-purpose flour, yeast, brown sugar, and caraway seed in separate bowl. Add heated mixture; stir until moistened, then beat well. Add remaining cup all-purpose flour; beat 2 minutes. Stir in enough rye flour to make a soft dough. Turn out onto lightly floured board or pastry cloth. Cover with bowl. Let rest 10 minutes. Knead 8 to 10 minutes, or until smooth and elastic. If dough is sticky, knead in additional rye flour. Shape into ball. Place in prepared bowl. Turn once to grease top. Cover and let rise in warm place, free from draft, 1 1/2 hours, or until double in bulk. Grease two 8-inch round cake pans. Punch dough down; divide in half. Shape each half into smooth ball. Place in prepared pans. Make 3 slashes 1/2 inch deep in top of each. Brush with butter. Cover and let rise in warm place, free from draft, 45 minutes, or until double in bulk. Preheat oven to 375°F. Bake 35 minutes, or until loaves sound hollow when lightly tapped. Transfer to wire racks to cool.

Bread can also be baked on a single greased baking sheet.

Anadama Bread _____ 2 loaves

1 cup water
1 cup milk
1/4 cup butter or margarine
6 to 6 1/2 cups Martha White
    All-Purpose Flour,
    divided

1 cup Martha White Self-
    Rising Corn Meal
2 teaspoons salt
2 packages (1/4 ounce each)
    active dry yeast
1/2 cup molasses

Grease large bowl; set aside. Heat water, milk, and butter in saucepan until very warm (120°F to 130°F). Combine 3 cups flour, corn meal, salt, and yeast in separate bowl. Add heated mixture and molasses; stir until blended. Add 3 cups flour; blend well. If dough is sticky, add remaining flour. Turn out onto floured board or pastry cloth. Cover with bowl. Let rest 10 minutes. Knead 8 to 10 minutes, or until smooth and elastic. Shape into ball. Place in prepared bowl. Turn once to grease top. Cover and let rise in warm place, free from draft, 1 to 1 1/2 hours, or until double in bulk. Grease two 9 × 5 × 3-inch loaf pans; set aside. Punch dough down; divide in half. Shape each half into a loaf. Place in prepared pans. Cover and let rise in warm place, free from draft, 1 hour, or until double in bulk. Preheat oven to 375°F. Bake 35 minutes, or until loaves sound hollow when lightly tapped. Transfer to wire racks to cool.

Light Dinner Rolls _____ 54 rolls

1 1/2 cups milk
1 1/2 cups water
1/2 cup butter or margarine
9 to 10 cups Martha White
    All-Purpose Flour,
    divided

1/2 cup sugar
4 teaspoons salt
2 packages (1/4 ounce each)
    active dry yeast
1 egg

Grease large bowl; set aside. Heat milk, water, and butter in saucepan until very warm (120°F to 130°F). Combine 3 cups flour, sugar, salt, and yeast in mixing bowl. Add heated mixture and egg; beat at high speed of electric mixer 2 minutes. Stir in enough remaining flour to make a soft dough. Turn out onto floured board or pastry cloth. Cover with bowl. Let rest 10 minutes. Knead 8 to 10 minutes, or until smooth and elastic. Shape into ball. Place in prepared bowl. Turn once to grease top. Cover and let rise in warm place, free from draft, 45 minutes, or until almost double in bulk. Grease 2 large baking sheets; set aside. Punch dough down; divide into 4 portions. Shape into rolls as desired (pages 12, 13). Place on prepared baking sheets. Cover and let rise in warm place, free from draft, 45 minutes, or until double in bulk. Preheat oven to 350°F. Bake 15 to 20 minutes, or until golden brown. Transfer to wire racks to cool.

Julekage (Norwegian Christmas Bread) _____ 2 loaves

1 recipe Sweet Yeast Dough
    (page 55)
1/2 teaspoon ground cardamom
1/3 cup finely chopped citron
2/3 cup raisins

Butter or margarine,
    melted
Confectioners Icing
    (page 44)

Prepare Sweet Yeast Dough, adding cardamom along with the egg. Grease two 9-inch round baking pans; set aside. After dough has risen, punch down. Knead in citron and raisins. Divide dough into 6 portions. Shape each portion into a ball. Place 3 of the balls, sides touching, in 1 of the prepared pans. Press tops of balls to flatten slightly. Brush with butter. Repeat with remaining 3 balls of dough. Cover and let rise in warm place, free from draft, 35 minutes, or until double in bulk. Preheat oven to 375°F. Bake 45 minutes, or until loaves sound hollow when lightly tapped. Cool slightly in pan. Frost while warm with Confectioners Icing. Decorate with candied fruit and nuts, if desired.

Sweet Yeast Dough ————— 1 recipe

2 packages (1/4 ounce each)
active dry yeast
1/2 cup warm water (105°F
to 115°F)
1/2 cup sugar
2 teaspoons salt

1/2 cup vegetable shortening
1/2 cup hot milk
2 eggs, lightly beaten
4 1/2 to 5 cups sifted
Martha White
All-Purpose Flour

Grease large bowl; set aside. Dissolve yeast in water in measuring cup; set aside. Combine sugar, salt, shortening, and milk in bowl. Cool to lukewarm. Add eggs; blend well. Add 2 cups flour; blend well. Stir in yeast mixture. Stir in enough remaining flour to make a soft dough. Turn out onto lightly floured board or pastry cloth. Cover with cloth. Let rest 10 minutes. Knead dough 8 to 10 minutes, or until smooth and elastic. Place in prepared bowl. Turn once to grease top. Cover and let rise in warm place, free from draft, 1 1/2 hours, or until double in bulk. Continue as directed in specific recipes such as Coconut Coffeecake (page 41), German Stollen (page 60), and Cinnamon Rolls (page 62).

Wheat Germ Batter Bread ——— 1 loaf

2 3/4 cups Martha White
All-Purpose Flour,
divided
1/2 cup plus 1 teaspoon wheat
germ, divided
2 packages (1/4 ounce each)
active dry yeast

1 1/2 teaspoons salt
1 cup very warm water (120°F
to 130°F)
1/4 cup honey
2 tablespoons butter or
margarine
1 egg, at room temperature

Combine 2 cups flour, 1/2 cup wheat germ, yeast, and salt in bowl. Add water, honey, butter, and egg; beat well. Add enough remaining flour to make a stiff batter. Cover and let rise in warm place, free from draft, 1 hour, or until double in bulk. Grease 9 × 5 × 3-inch loaf pan. Stir down batter. Spoon into prepared pan. Sprinkle with remaining teaspoon wheat germ. Cover with plastic wrap. Let rise in warm place, free from draft, 45 minutes, or until double in bulk. Preheat oven to 350°F. Bake 35 to 40 minutes, or until loaf sounds hollow when lightly tapped. Transfer to wire rack to cool.

Refrigerator Whole Wheat Bread _____ 2 loaves

2 cups milk	4 teaspoons salt
3/4 cup water	2 packages (1/4 ounce each)
1/4 cup butter or margarine	active dry yeast
4 cups Martha White	3 1/2 to 4 cups Martha White
All-Purpose Flour,	Whole Wheat Flour
divided	Vegetable oil
3 tablespoons brown sugar	

Heat milk, water and butter in saucepan until very warm (120°F to 130°F). Combine 3 cups all-purpose flour, sugar, salt, and yeast in mixing bowl. Gradually stir in heated mixture; beat at high speed of electric mixer 2 minutes, scraping bowl occasionally. Add remaining cup all-purpose flour; beat at high speed 2 minutes. Stir in enough whole wheat flour to make a stiff dough. Sprinkle board or pastry cloth with whole wheat flour. Turn dough out onto floured surface. Knead 8 to 10 minutes, or until smooth and elastic. Cover with plastic wrap, then a towel. Let rest 20 minutes. Grease two 9 × 5 × 3-inch loaf pans; set aside. Divide dough in half. Roll each half into 14 × 9-inch rectangle. Roll up, jelly-roll fashion, from long side; press ends under. Place loaves in prepared pans. Brush tops with oil. Cover with plastic wrap. Refrigerate at least 6 hours. When ready to bake, remove from refrigerator. Carefully remove plastic wrap. Let stand at room temperature 10 minutes. Preheat oven to 400°F. Bake 40 minutes, or until loaves sound hollow when lightly tapped. Transfer to wire rack to cool.

French Bread _____ 2 loaves

4 to 4 1/2 cups Martha White	1 1/2 cups very warm water
All-Purpose Flour,	(120°F to 130°F)
divided	1 tablespoon Martha White
2 teaspoons salt, divided	Corn Meal
1 package (1/4 ounce) active	1 egg
dry yeast	

Grease large bowl; set aside. Combine 2 cups flour, 1 1/2 teaspoons salt, and yeast in separate bowl; blend well. Add water; stir until moistened, then beat well. Gradually stir in enough remaining flour to make a stiff dough. Turn out onto lightly floured board or pastry cloth. Knead 8 to 10 minutes, or until smooth and elastic. Shape into ball. Place in prepared bowl. Turn once to grease top. Cover and let rise in warm place, free from draft, 1 hour, or until double in bulk. Grease two 17 × 14-inch baking sheets; sprinkle with corn meal; set aside. Punch dough down; divide in half. Roll each half out on lightly floured board or pastry cloth into 15 × 8-inch rectangle. Roll up tightly, jelly-roll fashion, from long side. Pinch ends to seal. Place diagonally, seam side down, on prepared baking sheets. Use a very sharp knife to make diagonal slashes 2 inches apart across tops of loaves. Cover and let rise in warm place, free from draft, 30 minutes, or until double in bulk. Preheat oven to 400°F. Combine egg and remaining 1/2 teaspoon salt in small dish; beat lightly with fork. Brush tops of loaves with egg wash. Bake 35 to 40 minutes, or until golden brown and loaves sound hollow when lightly tapped. Transfer to wire racks to cool.

If desired, shape half of the dough into French Bread loaf and use the other half to make hard rolls.

Leftover French Bread slices are delicious when used to make French toast.

Riz Biscuits
_____ 18 biscuits

2 1/2 cups sifted Martha White
    Self-Rising Flour
3 tablespoons sugar
1/4 teaspoon baking soda
1 package (1/4 ounce) active
    dry yeast

1/3 cup vegetable shortening
1 cup warm buttermilk
    (105°F to 115°F)
2 tablespoons butter or
    margarine, melted

Grease 2 baking sheets; set aside. Combine flour, sugar, baking soda, and yeast in bowl. Cut in shortening with pastry blender or 2 knives until mixture is consistency of coarse crumbs. Quickly stir in buttermilk until just moistened. Turn out onto lightly floured board or pastry cloth. Knead just until smooth. Roll out to 1/4-inch thickness. Cut into rounds with floured 2-inch biscuit cutter. Brush tops of rounds with butter. Stack 1 round on top of another to make a double biscuit. Repeat with remaining rounds. Place on prepared baking sheets. Cover and let rise in warm place, free from draft, 1 hour, or until double in bulk. Preheat oven to 375°F. Bake 12 to 15 minutes, or until golden brown.

Overnight
Oatmeal Bread _____ 1 loaf

1/2 cup uncooked quick oats	1 tablespoon butter or
1 cup boiling water	margarine
1 package (1/4 ounce) active	1 1/4 teaspoons salt
dry yeast	3 cups Martha White
1/3 cup warm water (105°F	All-Purpose Flour,
to 115°F)	divided
1/4 cup molasses or honey	

Combine oats and boiling water in bowl; let stand until just warm. Dissolve yeast in warm water. Keep in warm place until oat mixture cools. Stir yeast mixture into oat mixture. Add molasses, butter, and salt; blend thoroughly. Stir in 2 cups flour; blend well. Knead in remaining cup flour; blend well. Add additional flour, if necessary, to make a fairly stiff dough. Let rest 3 to 5 minutes. Grease 9 × 5 × 3-inch loaf pan; set aside. Turn dough out onto lightly floured board or pastry cloth. Knead 8 to 10 minutes, or until smooth. Shape into a loaf. Place in prepared pan. Lightly oil top of loaf. Cover and refrigerate at least 8 hours or up to 24 hours. Remove from refrigerator at least 10 minutes or up to 1 hour before baking. Preheat oven to 350°F. Bake 50 minutes, or until loaf sounds hollow when lightly tapped. Transfer to wire rack to cool.

Hot Muffin Rolls _____ 24 rolls

1 1/4 cups milk	1 package (1/4 ounce) active
1/2 cup vegetable shortening	dry yeast
3 1/4 cups Martha White	2 eggs, lightly beaten
All-Purpose Flour,	2 tablespoons butter or
divided	margarine, melted
1/4 cup sugar	

Heat milk and shortening in saucepan until very warm (120°F to 130°F). Combine 2 cups flour, sugar, and yeast in bowl. Stir in heated mixture. Add eggs and enough remaining flour to make a stiff batter. Beat until smooth. Cover and let rise in warm place, free from draft, 1 hour, or until double in bulk. Grease 24 muffin cups. Stir down batter. Fill prepared muffin cups two-thirds full. Brush tops with butter. Cover and let rise in warm place, free from draft, 30 minutes. Preheat oven to 375°F. Bake 25 minutes, or until golden brown. Serve hot.

Overnight Oatmeal Bread, Riz Biscuits (page 57) →

German Stollen _____ 3 stollen

1 recipe Sweet Yeast Dough (page 55)	Butter or margarine, softened
1/2 teaspoon grated lemon peel	Butter or margarine, melted
1/2 cup chopped pecans	Confectioners Icing (page 44)
1/2 cup raisins	
1/2 cup finely chopped mixed candied fruit	

Prepare Sweet Yeast Dough, kneading in lemon peel with last addition of flour. Grease 2 large baking sheets; set aside. After dough has risen, punch down. Knead in pecans, raisins, and candied fruit. Divide dough into thirds. Pat 1 third into 12 × 8-inch oval. Spread with softened butter. Fold in half lengthwise, bringing one side within 1/2 inch of opposite side. Press edges together lightly. Place on prepared baking sheet. Brush top with butter. Repeat with remaining 2 thirds. Cover and let rise in warm place, free from draft, 35 minutes, or until double in bulk. Preheat oven to 375°F. Bake 30 to 35 minutes, or until golden brown and loaves sound hollow when lightly tapped. Cool on baking sheets. Frost while warm with Confectioners Icing. Decorate with additional candied fruit and pecans, if desired.

Tearoom Refrigerator Rolls _____ About 48 rolls

1 cup diced raw potatoes	2 eggs, lightly beaten
1/2 cup vegetable shortening	Vegetable oil
1/3 cup sugar	2 tablespoons butter or margarine, melted
1 tablespoon salt	
1 package (1/4 ounce) active dry yeast	
5 to 6 cups Martha White All-Purpose Flour, divided	

Grease large bowl; set aside. Cook potatoes in unsalted water; reserve 1 1/2 cups potato water. Heat reserved potato water in saucepan until very warm (120°F to 130°F). Combine potato water, potatoes, and shortening in blender container; blend well; set aside. Combine sugar, salt, yeast, and 2 cups flour in separate bowl. Stir in potato mixture. Add eggs; blend well. Stir in enough remaining flour to make a fairly stiff dough. Turn out onto floured board or pastry cloth. Knead 8 to 10 minutes, or until

Bread

smooth and elastic. Place dough in prepared bowl. Turn once to grease top. Cover and let rise in warm place, free from draft, 2 hours, or until double in bulk. Punch dough down. Grease 2 large baking sheets; set aside. Shape dough into rolls as desired (pages 12, 13). Place on prepared baking sheets. Brush tops of rolls lightly with oil. Cover and let rise in warm place, free from draft, 45 minutes, or until double in bulk. Preheat oven to 400°F. Bake 15 to 20 minutes. Transfer to wire racks to cool. Brush tops with butter.

This dough keeps well. If you want to bake only a portion, cover and refrigerate remaining dough until ready to use, up to 4 days. Remove dough from refrigerator when ready to use. Punch down. Shape into rolls as desired. Place on prepared baking sheets. Cover and let rise in warm place, free from draft, 2 hours, or until double in bulk. Bake as directed above.

Onion Bread _____ 2 loaves

1 package (1/4 ounce) active
  dry yeast
1 cup warm water (105°F
  to 115°F)
3 1/4 to 3 3/4 cups sifted
  Martha White All-Purpose
  Flour, divided

2 teaspoons sugar
2 teaspoons salt
2 tablespoons butter or
  margarine, melted
2/3 cup chopped onions
2 teaspoons paprika

Grease large bowl; set aside. Dissolve yeast in water in separate bowl. Add 2 cups flour, sugar, and 1 teaspoon salt; stir until moistened, then beat well. Add enough remaining flour to make a soft dough. Turn out onto floured board or pastry cloth. Knead 8 to 10 minutes, or until smooth and elastic. Shape into ball. Place in prepared bowl. Turn once to grease top. Cover and let rise in warm place, free from draft, 1 hour, or until double in bulk. Grease two 9-inch round baking pans; set aside. Punch dough down; divide in half. Press each half into prepared pans. Brush tops with butter. Sprinkle onions evenly over tops. Use fingertips to press onions lightly into dough. Cover with plastic wrap. Let rise in warm place, free from draft, 40 minutes, or until double in bulk. Preheat oven to 450°F. Sprinkle each loaf with 1/2 teaspoon remaining salt and 1 teaspoon paprika. Bake 20 to 25 minutes, or until well browned and loaves sound hollow when lightly tapped. Transfer to wire racks to cool.

Cinnamon Rolls ⸺ About 48 rolls

1 recipe Sweet Yeast Dough
(page 55)
1/4 cup butter or margarine,
melted
1 cup sugar

1 tablespoon cinnamon
2 tablespoons milk
Confectioners Icing
(page 44)

Prepare Sweet Yeast Dough. After dough has risen, punch down. Let rest 10 minutes. Grease 4 8-inch round baking pans or 48 muffin cups; set aside. Divide dough into 4 portions. Roll out 1 portion into 12 × 6-inch rectangle. Brush with melted butter. Combine sugar and cinnamon in small bowl. Sprinkle one fourth of cinnamon-sugar mixture over rectangle. Roll up, jelly-roll fashion, from long side; seal edges. Cut into 1-inch slices. Place slices, cut sides down in prepared pans or muffin cups. Brush tops with milk. Repeat with remaining dough. Cover and let rise in warm place, free from draft, 45 minutes, or until double in bulk. Preheat oven to 350°F. Bake 25 minutes, or until golden brown. Turn out onto wire racks to cool. Frost warm rolls with Confectioners Icing.

Hot Cheese Rolls ⸺ 24 rolls

1 cup water
2 tablespoons vegetable
shortening
3 1/2 to 4 cups Martha White
All-Purpose Flour,
divided
1 tablespoon sugar
1/2 teaspoon salt

1 package (1/4 ounce) active
dry yeast
1 egg, lightly beaten
2 cups (8 ounces)
sharp Cheddar cheese,
shredded
2 tablespoons butter, melted

Grease large bowl; set aside. Heat water and shortening in saucepan until very warm (120°F to 130°F). Combine 2 cups flour, sugar, salt, and yeast in separate bowl. Add heated mixture; mix well. Stir in egg and cheese. Stir in enough remaining flour to make a soft dough. Turn out onto lightly floured board or pastry cloth. Cover with bowl. Let rest 10 minutes. Knead dough 8 to 10 minutes, or until elastic. Shape into ball. Place in prepared bowl. Turn once to grease top. Cover and let rise in warm place, free from draft, 1 hour, or until double in bulk. Grease 24 muffin cups. Punch dough down. Shape into Cloverleaf Rolls (pages 12, 13). Brush tops with melted butter. Cover and let rise in warm place, free from draft, 30 minutes, or until double in bulk. Preheat oven to 375°F. Bake 12 to 15 minutes, or until golden brown.

Country Corn Meal

There's something specially satisfying about the taste of cornbread. It's one of our best Southern traditions! So take a trip to corn meal country through these wonderful cornbreads, corn muffins, and specialties. Try Cornbread Dressing, to be sure, and Corn Meal Batter-Coated Fish (don't forget the Hush Puppies!).

Quick Corn Light Bread _____ 1 loaf

2 cups Martha White
  Self-Rising Corn Meal
1 cup sifted Martha White
  Self-Rising Flour

1/2 cup sugar
2 1/4 cups buttermilk
2 tablespoons vegetable
  shortening, melted

Preheat oven to 375°F. Grease and flour 9 × 5 × 3-inch pan; set aside. Combine corn meal, flour, and sugar in bowl. Add buttermilk and shortening; blend thoroughly. Pour into prepared pan. Let stand 15 minutes. Bake 45 minutes, or until golden brown. Cover pan with tea towel. Let stand until cool. Serve warm with butter or cool with sliced ham or turkey.

Sour Cream Cornbread _____ 12 servings

1 1/3 cups Martha White
  Self-Rising Corn Meal
1/3 cup sifted Martha White
  Self-Rising Flour
1 tablespoon sugar
1/4 teaspoon baking soda

1 egg, lightly beaten
1 cup (8 ounces) dairy
  sour cream
1/2 cup milk
2 tablespoons vegetable oil

Preheat oven to 400°F. Grease 9-inch square baking pan; preheat in oven. Combine corn meal, flour, sugar, and baking soda in bowl; set aside. Combine egg, sour cream, milk, and oil in separate bowl. Add to corn meal mixture; stir just until blended. Pour into hot pan. Bake 20 to 25 minutes, or until golden brown.

Follow above directions to make 12 muffins or corn sticks. Bake at 400°F 15 minutes.

Quick Cornbread Loaf _____ 1 loaf

2 packages (6 ounces each)
  Martha White Complete
  Buttermilk Cornbread
  Mix
2 tablespoons sugar

1 cup (8 ounces) dairy sour
  cream
3/4 cup milk
1 egg, lightly beaten

Preheat oven to 375°F. Grease 9 × 5 × 3-inch loaf pan; set aside. Combine all ingredients in bowl; stir until smooth. Pour into prepared pan. Bake 30 to 35 minutes, or until golden brown. Cool in pan 10 minutes. Turn out onto wire rack. Serve warm or cool.

Texas Cornbread _____ 12 servings

1 egg	2 tablespoons vegetable oil
1 cup Martha White	1/2 cup milk
Self-Rising Corn Meal	1 teaspoon sugar
1 can (8 1/2 ounces)	
cream-style corn	

Preheat oven to 450°F. Grease 8-inch square baking pan; set aside. Break egg into bowl and beat. Add remaining ingredients; stir until blended. Pour into prepared pan. Bake 20 to 25 minutes, or until golden brown.

Herbed Cornbread _____ 9 pieces

1 1/4 cups Martha White	1/2 teaspoon thyme
Self-Rising Corn Meal	1/2 teaspoon celery seed
3/4 cup sifted Martha White	2 eggs, lightly beaten
Self-Rising Flour	1 1/4 cups milk
1 teaspoon sugar	1/4 cup butter or margarine,
1/2 teaspoon marjoram	melted

Preheat oven to 425°F. Grease 9-inch square baking pan; preheat in oven. Combine corn meal, flour, sugar, marjoram, thyme, and celery seed in bowl. Combine eggs, milk, and butter in separate bowl. Add to flour mixture; stir just until blended. Pour into hot pan. Bake 25 minutes, or until golden brown. Cut into 3-inch pieces. Serve hot.

Butter Bite Hoecakes _____ About 14 cakes

1 cup Martha White	1 1/2 cups boiling water
Self-Rising Corn Meal	

Combine corn meal and boiling water in bowl. Stir lightly. Grease a large skillet or griddle. Preheat over moderate heat until a drop of water sizzles when dropped on skillet. Spoon batter, by tablespoonfuls, onto hot skillet. Cook over low heat until golden brown. Turn and cook other side until golden brown. Serve hot, spread with butter.

Country-Style Cornbread _____ 12 muffins, 16 sticks, or 1 skilletful

2 cups Martha White
   Self-Rising Corn Meal
1/2 teaspoon baking soda
1 1/2 cups buttermilk

1/4 cup bacon drippings or
   vegetable shortening,
   melted

Preheat oven to 450°F. Grease muffin cups, corn-stick mold, or 8-inch skillet; preheat in oven. Combine corn meal and baking soda in bowl. Add buttermilk and bacon drippings; blend thoroughly. Pour into hot pans. (Fill muffin cups and corn-stick pans two-thirds full.) Bake 20 to 25 minutes, or until golden brown.

Whole milk can be substituted for buttermilk by reducing amount to 1 1/3 cups and omitting baking soda.

Traditional Southern cornbread is brown and crusty. To make it this way, use black iron pans which have been greased and heated in the oven until they begin to smoke; batter should sizzle when poured into the pan.

Country-Style Cornbread →

Double-Good Cornbread _____ 16 squares

1 package (7 1/2 ounces)
  Martha White Corn
  Muffin Mix
1 can (17 ounces)
  cream-style corn

1/2 cup butter or margarine,
  melted
2 eggs, lightly beaten

Preheat oven to 350°F. Butter 8-inch square baking pan; set aside. Combine all ingredients in bowl; blend thoroughly. Spread in prepared pan. Bake 35 to 40 minutes, or until golden brown. Cut into 2-inch squares. Serve as a vegetable or bread.

Tex-Mex Cornbread _____ 12 servings

1 recipe Texas Cornbread
  (page 65)
1 cup (4 ounces) grated
  sharp Cheddar cheese

2 tablespoons chopped
  jalapeno peppers

Prepare Texas Cornbread recipe stirring cheese and peppers into batter.

Corn Cakes _____ 6 servings

1 cup Martha White
  Self-Rising Corn Meal
1/2 teaspoon sugar

3/4 cup milk
1 egg, lightly beaten
1 tablespoon vegetable oil

Combine corn meal, sugar, milk, egg, and oil in bowl; stir until smooth. Lightly grease 10-inch skillet and preheat over moderate heat until a drop of water sizzles when dropped on skillet. Pour 1/4 cup batter into skillet. Cook until golden brown on bottom; turn and cook other side until golden brown. Repeat with remaining batter. If batter becomes too thick, stir in a little additional milk. Serve with butter.

Egg Cornbread _____ 14 muffins, 18 sticks, or 1 skilletful

2 cups Martha White Self-Rising Corn Meal	1 1/4 cups milk
1 teaspoon sugar	1/4 cup bacon drippings or vegetable shortening, melted
2 eggs, lightly beaten	

Preheat oven to 450°F. Grease muffin cups, corn-stick mold, or 8-inch skillet; preheat in oven. Combine corn meal and sugar in bowl; set aside. Combine eggs, milk and bacon drippings in separate bowl. Add corn meal mixture; blend thoroughly. Pour into hot pans. (Fill muffin cups and corn-stick pans two-thirds full.) Bake 15 to 20 minutes, or until golden brown.

For buttermilk Egg Cornbread, substitute 1 1/2 cups buttermilk for whole milk and add 1/4 teaspoon baking soda.

Southern-Style Sausage Cornbread _____ 12 muffins, 18 sticks, or 1 skilletful

1/2 pound pork sausage	2 cups Martha White Self-Rising Corn Meal
1 egg	1 teaspoon sugar
1 1/4 cups milk	

Partially brown sausage in large skillet, breaking up with spoon. Drain; reserve 1/4 cup drippings. Preheat oven to 450°F. Grease muffin cups, corn-stick mold, or 10-inch skillet; preheat in oven. Combine egg, milk, and reserved drippings in bowl; stir with fork until blended. Stir in corn meal, sugar, and sausage; blend well. Pour into hot pans. Bake 25 to 30 minutes, or until golden brown.

If desired, 1/4 cup vegetable oil can be substituted for sausage drippings.

Corn Meal Waffles —— Eight 4 1/2-inch waffles

1 egg
1 1/2 cups milk
1 1/2 cups Martha White
    Self-Rising Corn Meal

1/4 cup vegetable oil
2 tablespoons sugar
    (optional)

Preheat waffle iron according to manufacturer's directions. Break egg into bowl and beat. Add remaining ingredients; beat until smooth. Bake in hot waffle iron. Serve hot with butter and syrup or topped with creamed chicken, if desired.

Bacon and Corn Meal Muffins ——————————— 12 muffins

1 cup sifted Martha White
    Self-Rising Flour
1 cup Martha White
    Self-Rising Corn Meal
3 tablespoons sugar
1/2 teaspoon baking soda
1 egg

1 cup buttermilk
1/4 cup vegetable shortening,
    melted, or vegetable
    oil
6 strips bacon, crisp-cooked
    and crumbled

Preheat oven to 425°F. Grease 12 muffin cups; set aside. Combine flour, corn meal, sugar, and baking soda in bowl; set aside. Break egg into small bowl; beat lightly with fork. Blend in buttermilk and shortening. Add buttermilk mixture and bacon to flour mixture; stir just until blended. Fill muffin cups two-thirds full. Bake 15 to 18 minutes, or until golden brown.

Today's spokesman for Martha White is the tremendously popular Tennessee Ernie Ford, whose "Goodness Gracious, It's Pea-Pickin' Good" slogan is a widely-known company trademark.

← Corn Meal Waffles

Corn Meal Coated
Chicken _____ 4 servings

1/4 cup butter or margarine	1/4 teaspoon poultry seasoning
1/4 cup Martha White	1/4 teaspoon salt
Self-Rising Flour	1/8 teaspoon thyme
1/4 cup Martha White	1/8 teaspoon pepper
Self-Rising Corn Meal	1 frying chicken (2 1/2 to
1/2 teaspoon paprika	3 pounds), cut up
1/2 teaspoon onion powder	

Preheat oven to 350°F. Melt butter in 13 × 9 × 2-inch baking pan in oven; set aside. Combine flour, corn meal, paprika, onion powder, poultry seasoning, salt, thyme, and pepper in plastic bag; set aside. Rinse chicken in cold water; pat dry with paper towels. Shake chicken, 2 pieces at a time, in corn meal mixture until thoroughly coated. Place chicken, skin side down, in pan with melted butter. Bake 1 hour, or until tender, turning with tongs or fork after 30 minutes.

To coat fish, omit poultry seasoning and thyme. Add 3/4 teaspoon lemon-pepper. Bake at 350°F 30 minutes, or until fish flakes easily with a fork, turning after 15 minutes.

Cheesy Corn Meal
Biscuits _____ 12 to 14 biscuits

1 1/2 cups sifted Martha White	1/3 cup vegetable shortening
Self-Rising Flour	1 cup (4 ounces) shredded
1/2 cup Martha White	Cheddar cheese
Self-Rising Corn Meal	3/4 cup milk

Preheat oven to 450°F. Grease baking sheet; set aside. Combine flour and corn meal in bowl. Cut in shortening with pastry blender or 2 knives until mixture is consistency of coarse crumbs. Stir in cheese. Add milk; stir with fork until dough leaves sides of bowl. Turn out onto lightly floured board or pastry cloth. Knead until smooth. Roll out to 1/2-inch thickness. Cut into rounds with floured 2-inch biscuit cutter. Place on prepared baking sheet. Bake 10 to 12 minutes, or until golden brown.

Corn Meal Batter-Coated Fish _____ 6 servings

2 pounds fish fillets, cut
  into serving-size pieces
1/3 cup Martha White
  All-Purpose Flour
Oil for deep-fat frying
1/2 cup Martha White
  Self-Rising Flour

1/2 cup Martha White
  Self-Rising Corn Meal
1/4 teaspoon salt
1 egg, lightly beaten
2/3 cup milk
1 tablespoon vegetable oil

Rinse fish in cold water; pat dry with paper towels. Place all-purpose flour in shallow dish. Coat fish evenly with flour; set aside. Heat oil for deep-fat frying to 350°F. Combine self-rising flour, corn meal, and salt in small bowl. Combine egg, milk, and vegetable oil in bowl. Gradually add flour mixture, beating until smooth. Dip floured fish into batter to coat. Deep fry fish, a few pieces at a time, 4 to 6 minutes, or until golden brown, turning to brown evenly. Drain on paper towels. To keep fish warm until all pieces are cooked, place in shallow pan in 300°F oven.

If you prefer a lighter coating, simply place about 3/4 cups Martha White Self-Rising Corn Meal in a shallow dish. Coat fish evenly. Deep fry as directed above.

Hush Puppies _____ 16 servings

2 1/4 cups Martha White
  Self-Rising Corn Meal
3 tablespoons Martha White
  Self-Rising Flour

3 tablespoons finely chopped
  onion
1 egg, lightly beaten
1 cup milk or water

Combine corn meal, flour, and onion in bowl; mix lightly. Add egg; blend well. Gradually beat in milk until smooth. Drop batter by tablespoonfuls into hot fat in which fish has been fried. Fry until golden brown. Drain on paper towels. Serve spread with butter.

Traditional with fish, of course, Hush Puppies are fine with many dishes. Prepare in hot fat used to cook chicken or veal, for example.

Cornbread
Dressing ——————————— For one 5-pound chicken

Giblets from chicken
2 cups water
3/4 cup butter or margarine
1 cup finely chopped celery
1/4 cup finely chopped onion
4 cups toasted dry bread
  cubes or crumbled
  biscuits

3 cups crumbled cornbread
2 teaspoons salt
1 teaspoon poultry
  seasoning
1/2 teaspoon pepper

Combine giblets and water in saucepan. Cook until giblets are no longer pink. Reserve 2 cups broth. (Set giblets aside; chop and add to gravy, if desired.) Melt butter in heavy skillet. Sauté celery and onion in butter until onion is transparent. Add bread cubes, cornbread, and seasonings. Pour reserved broth over ingredients in skillet; stir lightly to blend. Stuff cavity. Truss, if directed in recipe. Roast as directed.

Dressing can be baked separately. Preheat oven to 350°F. Use hands to shape dressing into cones or balls. Place in baking pan. Cover with aluminum foil. Bake 20 minutes. Remove foil. Bake 10 minutes.

Going to the Fair

"Simple Simon met a pieman . . ." And what did he discover? The creamiest, fruitiest, nuttiest pies you've ever tasted. Begin the best of pies with our delicate pastry, fill them with kitchen-tested fillings, and top them with our Perfect Meringue or sweetened whipped cream.

Basic Pastry Recipes

Use either Martha White All-Purpose Flour or Martha White Self-Rising Flour for pastry crusts. If using Self-Rising Flour, omit salt from pastry ingredients. For pies with thin filling, such as Pecan, Lemon, Rhubarb, or Chess Pie, we recommend using only Martha White All-Purpose Flour.

One-Crust 9-inch Pie

1 cup sifted Martha White All-Purpose Flour	1/3 cup vegetable shortening
1/2 teaspoon salt	2 1/2 to 3 tablespoons cold water

Combine flour and salt in bowl. Cut in half of the shortening with pastry blender or 2 knives until mixture is consistency of coarse crumbs. Cut in remaining shortening until mixture is consistency of small peas. Sprinkle a small amount of water over mixture; stir with fork. Repeat with remaining water until dough is moist enough to form a ball but not sticky. Shape into ball.

Flatten dough on floured board or pastry cloth. Roll gently with rolling pin outward from center to 1/8-inch thickness. Roll into circle about 1 inch larger than pie pan. Fold dough in half. Transfer to pie pan; unfold and fit loosely into pan without stretching dough. Use small ball of excess dough to press gently into bottom and sides of pan. If dough tears, patch by moistening with a little water and pressing torn edges together. Trim overhang with kitchen shears to 1 inch. Fold overhang under, then press to form stand-up edge.

Preheat oven to 475°F. Prick bottom of crust thoroughly with fork dipped in flour. Bake 8 to 10 minutes, or until golden brown.

Two-Crust 9-inch Pie

2 cups sifted Martha White All-Purpose Flour	2/3 cup vegetable shortening
1 teaspoon salt	4 1/2 to 5 tablespoons cold water

Combine flour and salt in bowl. Cut in half of the shortening with pastry blender or 2 knives until mixture is consistency of coarse crumbs. Cut in remaining shortening until mixture is consistency of small peas. Sprinkle a small amount of water over mixture; stir with fork. Repeat with remaining water until dough is moist enough to form a ball but not sticky. Shape into ball.

Divide dough in half. Roll bottom crust as for one-crust pastry. Trim flush with rim of pie pan. Pour filling into crust. Moisten edge of bottom crust with water. Roll out remaining dough 1 inch larger than pan. Fold in half. Carefully place on top of filling; unfold. Press edges together, tucking top pastry under edge of bottom pastry. Flute edges. Cut slits in top to allow steam to escape. Bake as directed.

To Flute Edge: Press knuckle of middle finger into inside edge of dough while pressing thumb and index fingers of other hand from other side. Repeat procedure to flute entire edge.

Decorative Tops for Pies

Woven Lattice Top

Trim bottom crust 1/2 inch larger than pie pan. Cut top pastry into 1/2-inch wide strips with sharp knife or pastry wheel. Lay 5 to 7 strips across top of filling, about 1 inch apart. Fold back every other strip. Lay 5 to 7 strips crosswise across first strips. Pull first strips over second strips. Repeat for remaining strips. Trim ends. Bring edge of bottom crust up over strips. Press to make stand-up edge. Flute edge.

Quick Lattice Top

Cut strips as for woven lattice top (above). Lay strips 1 inch across entire top of pie. Finish by placing strips crosswise across top of first strips. Trim ends. Make stand-up edge and flute as above.

Twisted Lattice

Cut strips 1/2 inch wide. Beginning in center of pie, lay strips at 1-inch intervals, twisting strips as they are laid down. Place remaining strips in opposite direction to form diamond pattern. Moisten edges and press to seal to rim.

Woven Lattice Top

Quick Lattice Top

Twisted Lattice Top

77

FIRST

Blue Ribbon Cherry Pie _____ 1 pie

Pastry for 2-crust pie
(page 76)
1 cup sugar
3 tablespoons cornstarch
1/8 teaspoon salt
1 can (16 ounces) cherries,
drained; reserve
1/2 cup juice

1/4 teaspoon red food coloring
1 tablespoon butter or
margarine
1/4 teaspoon almond extract

Line 8-inch pie pan with bottom pastry; trim overhang to 1/2 inch. Combine sugar, cornstarch, and salt in 2-quart saucepan. Add cherries, reserved juice, and food coloring; cook over moderate heat until thick, stirring constantly. Remove from heat. Add butter and almond extract. Let stand until cool. Roll out dough for top crust; cut into strips with knife or pastry wheel; set aside. Preheat oven to 425°F. Pour filling into pie shell. Weave lattice pattern over filling (page 77). Seal and flute edge. Bake 10 minutes. Reduce oven temperature to 350°F. Bake 35 minutes, or until golden brown and juices begin to bubble. Cool in pan on wire rack.

Tips for Perfect Pies

- When making pastry dough, work quickly, handle the dough as little as possible, and avoid overmixing.
- Use a pastry blender or 2 knives to cut shortening into flour.
- A pastry cloth and stockinet-covered rolling pin are recommended for rolling out dough. Since less flour is used to roll the dough out, a more flaky and tender pastry is produced.
- Use the proper size pie pan for the recipe. If the size is not shown on the bottom, measure across from inside of rim.
- Use dull metal or glass pie pans for best results.
- To ensure a tender pastry, chill dough in refrigerator before rolling out, especially if room is warm.
- Preheat oven to temperature called for in recipe.
- To prevent pie juices from running over pie pan, place a small funnel or 4-inch piece of uncooked macaroni in center of pie before baking.

← Blue Ribbon Cherry Pie

Black Walnut Pie _____ 1 pie

3 eggs, lightly beaten
1 cup firmly packed brown
  sugar
1/8 teaspoon salt
1 cup dark corn syrup
3 tablespoons butter or
  margarine, melted

1 teaspoon vanilla
1 unbaked 9-inch pie shell
  (page 76), chilled
1 cup black walnuts,
  coarsely chopped

Preheat oven to 350°F. Combine eggs, brown sugar, salt, corn syrup, butter, and vanilla in bowl; blend well. Pour into pie shell. Sprinkle black walnuts over top. Bake 1 hour, or until knife inserted in center comes out clean. Cool in pan on wire rack.

Fresh Peach Pie _____ 1 pie

Pastry for 2-crust pie
  (page 76)
3 cups sliced peeled fresh
  peaches
3/4 to 1 cup sugar

1/4 cup Martha White
  All-Purpose Flour
1/2 teaspoon cinnamon
Dash salt
1 tablespoon butter

Line 8-inch pie pan with bottom pastry; trim overhang to 1/2 inch. Roll out dough for top crust; set aside. Preheat oven to 425°F. Place peaches in large bowl. Combine sugar, flour, cinnamon, and salt in small bowl. Sprinkle sugar mixture over peaches; toss lightly to mix. Arrange peaches in pie shell. Dot with butter. Cover with top crust. Cut slits in top to allow steam to escape. Seal and flute edge. Bake 35 to 40 minutes, or until golden brown and juices begin to bubble. Cool in pan on wire rack.

Fresh Blueberry Pie

Prepare pastry and filling as for Fresh Peach Pie, substituting 3 cups fresh blueberries and adding 2 teaspoons lemon juice.

Fresh Cherry Pie

Prepare pastry and filling as for Fresh Peach Pie, substituting 3 cups pitted cherries and adding 1/4 teaspoon almond extract.

Fresh Blackberry Pie

Prepare pastry and filling as for Fresh Peach Pie, substituting 3 cups blackberries.

Lemon Meringue Pie _____ 1 pie

1/3 cup Martha White Self-Rising Flour	3 egg yolks, lightly beaten
1 1/4 cups sugar, divided	2 1/4 cups water
3 tablespoons cornstarch	1 tablespoon butter or margarine
1/4 teaspoon salt	1 baked 9-inch pie shell (page 76)
1 tablespoon grated lemon peel	Perfect Meringue (page 87)
1/3 cup lemon juice	

Combine flour, 1/4 cup sugar, cornstarch, salt, and lemon peel in small bowl; blend well. Stir in lemon juice and egg yolks; set aside. Combine remaining cup sugar and water in small saucepan; bring to a boil over high heat, stirring frequently. When mixture reaches full boil, remove from heat. Slowly stir about 1 cup sugar-water mixture into egg yolk mixture; return all to saucepan. Bring mixture to a boil over medium-high heat, stirring constantly. Boil 3 minutes, stirring constantly. Remove from heat. Stir in butter; let stand until cool. Preheat oven to 400°F. Pour filling into pie shell. Spoon mounds of Perfect Meringue around outer edge of filling. Spread carefully around edge, being certain that meringue touches inner edge of crust. Spoon remaining meringue over center of filling; spread to border. Bake 8 to 10 minutes, or until peaks are golden brown. Cool in pan on wire rack away from draft.

Fresh Strawberry Pie _____ 1 pie

1 quart strawberries, hulled, divided	Milk or cream
1 cup sugar	1 baked 9-inch pie shell (page 76)
3 tablespoons cornstarch	
1 package (3 ounces) cream cheese, at room temperature	

Place 2 cups strawberries in bowl. Mash with fork. Measure strawberries and juice. Add water, if necessary, to equal 1 1/2 cups. Place in saucepan; add sugar and cornstarch. Bring to a boil over moderate heat, stirring constantly. Boil about 2 minutes. Remove from heat; set aside to cool. Place cream cheese in small bowl. Add a little milk; blend until smooth. Spread over bottom of pie shell. Halve or slice remaining strawberries. Arrange over cream cheese. Pour glaze evenly over strawberries. Refrigerate at least 2 hours. Serve topped with sweetened whipped cream.

Tennessee Apple Pie _____ 1 pie

Pastry for 2 crust pie
(page 76)
6 cups (6 or 7 medium)
   sliced peeled tart
   apples
2/3 cup sugar
1/4 cup firmly packed brown
   sugar
1/2 cup orange juice
1 egg white, lightly beaten
1/4 teaspoon nutmeg
1/4 teaspoon cinnamon
2 tablespoons butter or
   margarine

Line 9-inch pie pan with bottom pastry; trim overhang to 1/2 inch. Roll out dough for top crust; set aside. Combine apples, sugars, and orange juice in large saucepan. Add enough water to just cover apples. Cook over moderate heat until apples are tender. Remove apples with slotted spoon; set aside. Bring syrup to a boil; boil until slightly thickened, stirring constantly. Preheat oven to 425°F. Brush bottom pastry with part of egg white. Arrange apples in pie shell. Pour syrup over top. Sprinkle with nutmeg and cinnamon. Dot with butter. Place top crust over filling. Seal and crimp edges. Brush top with remaining egg white. Sprinkle lightly with sugar. Bake 40 minutes, or until golden brown.

Blueberry Pie _____ 1 pie

Pastry for 2-crust pie
(page 76)
1 can (14 ounces) water-
   packed blueberries
2/3 cup sugar
2 tablespoons cornstarch
1 tablespoon Martha White
   All-Purpose Flour
1/4 teaspoon salt
1 tablespoon butter or
   margarine
2 teaspoons lemon juice

Line 8-inch pie pan with bottom pastry; trim overhang to 1/2 inch. Preheat oven to 400°F. Drain blueberries; reserve juice. Combine sugar, cornstarch, flour, and salt in 2-quart saucepan; blend well. Stir in reserved juice. Bring to a boil over medium-high heat, stirring constantly. Remove from heat. Stir in blueberries, butter, and lemon juice. Roll out dough for top crust. Pour filling into pie shell. Cover with top crust. Cut slits in top to allow steam to escape. (If desired, cut pastry into strips and weave lattice pattern over filling, page 77.) Seal and flute edge. Bake 35 to 40 minutes. Cool in pan on wire rack. Serve warm.

Tennessee Apple Pie →

Peanut Butter Pie _____ 1 pie

1/2 cup sifted confectioners
    sugar
1/4 cup chunky peanut butter
1 baked 9-inch pie shell
    (page 76)
2/3 cup sugar, divided
2 tablespoons cornstarch
1 tablespoon Martha White
    All-Purpose Flour

1/4 teaspoon salt
2 1/4 cups milk, divided
3 egg yolks, lightly beaten
1 tablespoon butter or
    margarine
1 teaspoon vanilla
Perfect Meringue (page 87)

Combine confectioners sugar and peanut butter in small bowl; blend well. Sprinkle half of peanut butter mixture over bottom of pie shell. Combine 1/3 cup sugar, cornstarch, flour, and salt in small bowl; blend thoroughly. Add 1/4 cup milk and egg yolks; blend well; set aside. Combine remaining 1/3 cup sugar and 2 cups milk in saucepan. Bring to a boil over medium-high heat, stirring constantly. Remove from heat. Slowly stir about 1 cup hot milk mixture into egg yolk mixture; return all to saucepan. Bring to a boil over medium-high heat, stirring constantly. Boil 4 minutes, or until thickened. Remove from heat. Stir in butter and vanilla. Let stand until cool. Preheat oven to 400°F. Pour filling into pie shell. Spoon mounds of Perfect Meringue around outer edge of filling. Spread carefully around edge, being certain that meringue touches inner edge of crust. Spoon remaining meringue over center of filling; spread to border. Sprinkle remaining peanut butter mixture over meringue. Bake 8 to 10 minutes, or until peaks are golden brown. Cool in pan on wire rack away from draft.

Cranberry-Orange Pie _____ 1 pie

1 can (16 ounces) whole
    berry cranberry sauce
1/2 cup firmly packed brown
    sugar
1 package (3 ounces) orange
    gelatin

1/2 pint heavy cream, whipped
1/2 cup chopped nuts
1 baked 9-inch pie shell
    (page 76)

Combine cranberry sauce and brown sugar in saucepan; cook over moderate heat, stirring frequently, until mixture begins to bubble. Remove from heat. Add gelatin; stir until dissolved. Let stand until as thick as an unbeaten egg white. Fold in whipped cream and nuts. Spoon into pie shell. Refrigerate 3 to 4 hours, or until firm.

Swiss Chocolate Pie _____ 1 pie

1 cup plus 2 tablespoonfuls sugar, divided	12 large marshmallows
1/2 cup Martha White Self-Rising Flour	2 tablespoons butter or margarine
2 cups milk	1 teaspoon vanilla
2 squares (1 ounce each) unsweetened chocolate	1 baked 9-inch pie shell (page 76)
	1/2 pint heavy cream

Combine 1 cup sugar and flour in saucepan. Gradually add milk, stirring constantly. Cook over moderate heat, stirring constantly, until mixture is thick and mounds slightly. Add chocolate and marshmallows; cook and stir until melted. Remove from heat. Stir in butter and vanilla. Let stand until cool. Pour into pie shell. Refrigerate 2 to 3 hours. Before serving, beat cream at high speed of electric mixer in small mixing bowl until stiff peaks form, gradually adding remaining 2 tablespoons sugar. Garnish pie with sweetened whipped cream.

Dorothy's Caramel Pie _____ 1 pie

1 3/4 cups sugar, divided	2 tablespoons butter or margarine
1/2 cup Martha White Self-Rising Flour	1 baked 9-inch pie shell (page 76)
3 egg yolks	Perfect Meringue (page 87)
2 cups milk	

Combine 3/4 cup sugar and flour in saucepan; set aside. Place egg yolks in small bowl; beat lightly with fork. Stir in milk. Stir milk mixture into sugar mixture. Cook over moderate heat, stirring constantly, until custard thickens slightly. Remove from heat; set aside. Place remaining cup sugar in heavy skillet. Cook over moderate heat, stirring with wooden spoon, until golden brown and caramelized. Remove from heat. Stir rapidly into custard. Return to moderate heat. Cook and stir until thick and smooth. Remove from heat. Stir in vanilla and butter. Let stand until cool. Pour filling into pie shell. Preheat oven to 400°F. Spoon mounds of Perfect Meringue around outer edge of filling. Spread carefully around edge, being certain that meringue touches inner edge of crust. Spoon remaining meringue over center of filling; spread to border. Bake 8 to 10 minutes, or until peaks are golden brown. Cool in pan on wire rack away from draft.

Black Bottom Pie _____ 1 pie

1 cup sugar, divided	1 envelope unflavored
1 1/2 tablespoons cornstarch	gelatin
4 eggs, separated	1/4 cup cold water
2 cups hot milk	1/4 teaspoon cream of tartar
1 1/2 squares (1 1/2 ounces)	1 tablespoon brandy extract
semisweet chocolate,	1/2 pint heavy cream
melted	2 tablespoons shaved
1 teaspoon vanilla	chocolate
1 baked 9-inch pie shell	
(page 76)	

Combine 1/2 cup sugar and cornstarch in small bowl; set aside. Place egg yolks in saucepan; beat with electric mixer until lemon-colored. Gradually stir in milk. Add sugar mixture. Cook over moderate heat, stirring constantly, until custard coats back of spoon. Pour 1 cup custard into large measuring cup. Stir in chocolate and vanilla. Pour into pie shell. Refrigerate until cool. Dissolve gelatin in cold water. Stir into remaining custard in saucepan. Refrigerate until cool. Place egg whites in small mixing bowl. Add cream of tartar. Beat at low speed of electric mixer until foamy. Add 6 tablespoons sugar, a little at a time, beating until soft peaks form. Gently fold into custard-gelatin mixture. Stir in brandy extract. Pour over chocolate layer in pie shell. Refrigerate until set. Beat cream at high speed of electric mixer in small mixing bowl until stiff peaks form, gradually beating in remaining 2 tablespoons sugar. Garnish pie with sweetened whipped cream and shaved chocolate.

Almond Crunch Pie _____ 1 pie

1/2 pint heavy cream	1/2 cup chopped pecans
1 cup sugar	1 teaspoon almond extract
1 cup Coconut Drop Cookie	1 baked 9-inch pie shell
crumbs (page 96)	(page 76)
1/2 cup flaked coconut,	
toasted	

Beat cream at high speed of electric mixer in large mixing bowl until stiff peaks form, gradually beating in sugar. Reserve one-third of whipped cream. Fold cookie crumbs, coconut, pecans, and almond extract into remaining whipped cream. Spoon mixture into pie shell. Spread reserved whipped cream evenly over top. Refrigerate at least 1 hour.

Perfect Meringue ———————— Topping for 1 pie

3 egg whites, at room temperature	1/4 teaspoon cream of tartar
	6 tablespoons sugar

Preheat oven to 400°F. Place egg whites in small mixing bowl. Add cream of tartar. Beat at low speed of electric mixer until foamy. Add sugar, a little at a time, beating at medium-high speed until soft peaks form. Spoon mounds of meringue around outer edge of pie filling. Spread carefully around edge, being certain that meringue touches inner edge of crust. Spoon remaining meringue over center of filling; spread to border. Bake 8 to 10 minutes, or until peaks are golden brown. Cool pie in pan on wire rack.

Cranberry-Apple-Mince Pie ——— 1 pie

Pastry for 2-crust pie (page 76)	1/2 cup whole berry cranberry sauce
2 cups mincemeat	1/2 cup currants or raisins
1 cup chopped peeled apples	

Preheat oven to 425°F. Line 8-inch pie pan with bottom pastry; trim overhang to 1/2 inch. Combine mincemeat, apples, cranberry sauce, and currants in large bowl; blend well. Roll out dough for top crust; cut into strips with knife or pastry wheel; set aside. Pour filling into pie shell. Weave lattice pattern over filling (page 77). Seal and flute edge. Bake 30 minutes, or until golden brown. Cool in pan on wire rack.

Pumpkin Pie ———————————————— 1 pie

1 1/3 cups sugar	1/2 teaspoon cinnamon
1/3 cup butter or margarine	1/4 teaspoon ginger
1 tablespoon Martha White Self-Rising Corn Meal	1/4 teaspoon nutmeg
	1/8 teaspoon ground cloves
1/3 cup half-and-half	1 teaspoon vanilla
3 eggs	1 unbaked 9-inch pie shell
1 cup canned pumpkin	(page 76), chilled
1/2 teaspoon salt	

Preheat oven to 350°F. Cream sugar and butter with electric mixer in mixing bowl until light and fluffy. Add corn meal and half-and-half; blend well. Add eggs, 1 at a time, beating well after each addition. Add pumpkin, spices, and vanilla; blend well. Pour into pie shell. Bake 50 minutes, or until pie is well browned and knife inserted about 1 inch from edge comes out clean. (Center will not be completely set.) Cool in pan on wire rack.

Vanilla Cream Pie _____ 1 pie

2/3 cup sugar, divided	3 egg yolks, lightly beaten
2 tablespoons cornstarch	1 tablespoon butter or
1 tablespoon Martha White	margarine
All-Purpose Flour	1 teaspoon vanilla
1/4 teaspoon salt	1 baked 9-inch pie shell
2 1/4 cups milk, divided	(page 76)

Combine 1/3 cup sugar, cornstarch, flour, and salt in small bowl. Stir in 1/4 cup milk and egg yolks; set aside. Combine remaining 1/3 cup sugar and 2 cups milk in saucepan. Bring to a boil over high heat, stirring constantly. When mixture reaches full boil, remove from heat. Slowly stir 1 cup milk mixture into egg yolk mixture. Return all to saucepan. Bring to a boil over moderate heat, stirring constantly. Boil 5 minutes, stirring constantly. Remove from heat. Stir in butter and vanilla. Let stand until cool. Pour into pie shell. Refrigerate at least 2 hours. Top with sweetened whipped cream or Perfect Meringue (page 87).

Chocolate Cream Pie

Prepare Vanilla Cream Pie filling, increasing sugar to 1 cup and melting 2 squares (1 ounce each) unsweetened chocolate in milk-sugar mixture.

Coconut Cream Pie

Prepare Vanilla Cream Pie filling, adding 1 cup shredded coconut. Top with Perfect Meringue (page 87). Sprinkle with 1/3 cup shredded coconut. Preheat oven to 400°F. Bake 8 to 10 minutes, or until peaks are golden brown and coconut is toasted.

Banana Cream Pie

Prepare Vanilla Cream Pie filling. Slice 2 bananas; arrange in bottom of pie shell. Add filling. Garnish with sweetened whipped cream.

The Cookie Jar

Listen for the satisfying sound of the lid of the cookie jar as it's slowly lifted and put back in place. From traditional favorites, like our Peanut Butter Cookies, to happy Holiday Fruit Bars, these finger-lickin' treats will delight your cookie jar crowd. Keep plenty on hand. They're going to disappear as fast as it takes you to fill the jar.

Chocolate Pinwheels _____ About 60 cookies

2/3 cup sugar
1/2 cup vegetable shortening
1 egg
1 tablespoon milk
2 cups sifted Martha White
  Self-Rising Flour

1 square (1 ounce)
  unsweetened chocolate,
  melted

Cream sugar and shortening with electric mixer in mixing bowl until light and fluffy. Add egg and milk; blend thoroughly. Gradually blend in flour. Divide dough in half. Add chocolate to 1 half; blend thoroughly. Refrigerate both halves 1 hour, or until firm enough to roll out. Roll out each half on floured waxed paper into 12 × 10-inch rectangle, 1/8 inch thick. Invert plain dough over chocolate dough; remove waxed paper. Roll up, jelly-roll fashion, from long side. Wrap in plastic wrap. Refrigerate overnight. Preheat oven to 375°F. Carefully remove plastic wrap. Cut roll into 1/8-inch thick slices. Place slices on ungreased baking sheets. Bake 10 minutes. Transfer to wire racks to cool.

Unsliced cookie rolls can be frozen wrapped in aluminum foil 3 to 4 weeks. Remove from freezer and thaw partially before slicing.

Fruitcake Cookies _____ 48 to 60 cookies

1 1/2 cups sifted Martha White
  Self-Rising Flour
1/2 teaspoon baking soda
1/2 teaspoon allspice
1/2 cup firmly packed brown
  sugar
1/2 cup butter or margarine
2 eggs

1/4 cup milk
1 cup chopped candied
  cherries
1 cup chopped dates
1 cup (3 slices) chopped
  candied pineapple
1/3 cup raisins
3 cups chopped nuts

Preheat oven to 350°F. Lightly grease 2 large baking sheets; set aside. Combine flour, baking soda, and allspice in bowl; set aside. Cream brown sugar and butter with electric mixer in mixing bowl until light and fluffy. Add eggs; blend well. Alternately beat in flour mixture and milk, blending well after each addition, and scraping bowl with rubber spatula. Add fruit and nuts; blend well. Drop by teaspoonfuls onto prepared baking sheets. Bake 10 to 12 minutes, or until golden brown. Transfer to wire racks to cool.

Chocolate Pinwheels, Party Pecan Balls (page 92), Fruitcake Cookies, →
Iced Lemon Butter Bars (page 92)

Party Pecan Balls _____ About 66 cookies

1 1/4 cups confectioners sugar,
   sifted, divided
1/2 cup butter or margarine,
   softened
1 teaspoon vanilla

1 cup sifted Martha White
   All-Purpose Flour
1/8 teaspoon salt
1 cup finely chopped pecans

Cream 1/4 cup confectioners sugar and butter with electric mixer in mixing bowl until smooth. Add vanilla; blend well. Add flour and salt; blend well. Stir in pecans. Cover with aluminum foil. Refrigerate about 1 hour. Preheat oven to 350°F. Lightly grease 2 baking sheets. Shape dough into 1/2-inch balls. Place on prepared baking sheets. Bake 15 minutes, or until lightly browned. Remove from baking sheets. Carefully roll each ball in remaining cup confectioners sugar to coat. Cool on wire racks. Roll again in confectioners sugar. Store in airtight container.

Back in 1899, a man in Nashville, Tennessee, named one of his products at the Royal Flour Mill for his three-year-old daughter, Martha White Lindsey. Today, good cooks all over the country still "Bake Right with Martha White."

Iced Lemon Butter Bars _____ 16 bars

1 1/3 cups sifted Martha White
   All-Purpose Flour
1 cup sugar, divided
1/2 cup butter, softened
2 eggs

2 tablespoons Martha White
   All-Purpose Flour
1 teaspoon grated lemon peel
2 tablespoons lemon juice
   Confectioners sugar

Preheat oven to 350°F. Combine 1 1/3 cups sifted flour, 1/4 cup sugar and butter in bowl; blend until dough forms a ball. Pat into ungreased 9-inch square baking pan. Bake 15 minutes. Combine eggs, remaining 3/4 cup sugar, 2 tablespoons flour, lemon peel, and lemon juice in bowl; blend well. Pour over partially baked crust. Bake 18 to 20 minutes, or until filling is set. Sift confectioners sugar over top. Cool in pan on wire rack. Cut into bars.

Almond Slice and Bake Cookies _____ About 40 cookies

1 cup sugar	3 cups sifted Martha White
1 cup butter or margarine,	All-Purpose Flour
softened	1/2 teaspoon salt
2 eggs	1/2 cup ground almonds
1 teaspoon almond extract	70 whole almonds

Combine sugar, butter, eggs, and almond extract in mixing bowl; beat with electric mixer until blended. Gradually add flour; blend well. Add salt and ground almonds; blend well. Cover and refrigerate about 1 1/2 hours. Divide dough into thirds. Shape each third into 6 1/2 × 1 1/2-inch roll. Wrap in aluminum foil. Refrigerate at least 3 hours or overnight. Preheat oven to 400°F. Cut rolls into 1/2-inch thick slices. Place on ungreased baking sheets. Flatten each cookie with bottom of small glass dipped in flour. Press a whole almond in center of each. Bake 8 to 10 minutes, or until golden brown around edges. Transfer to wire racks to cool.

Pecan Slice and Bake Cookies

Follow recipe for Almond Slice and Bake Cookies, substituting chopped pecans for ground almonds and vanilla for almond extract. Top each cookie with pecan half.

Nuts can be ground in blender or food processor.

Peanut Butter Cookies ___ About 48 cookies

1/2 cup sugar	1 egg
1/2 cup firmly packed brown	1 1/2 teaspoons vanilla
sugar	1 1/4 cups sifted Martha White
1/2 cup butter or margarine	Self-Rising Flour
1/3 cup peanut butter	

Preheat oven to 350°F. Cream sugars, butter, and peanut butter with electric mixer in mixing bowl until light and fluffy. Add egg and vanilla; blend well. Gradually beat in flour until thoroughly blended. Shape dough into 1-inch balls. Place on ungreased baking sheets. Use fork dipped in flour to flatten tops of balls in crisscross pattern. Bake 12 minutes, or until golden brown. Transfer to wire racks to cool.

Apricot Bars _____ 24 bars

1 cup sugar
1 cup butter
2 egg yolks
2 cups sifted Martha White
  All-Purpose Flour

1 cup chopped nuts
1/2 teaspoon salt
Apricot Filling (below)

Preheat oven to 325°F. Grease 9-inch square baking pan; set aside. Cream sugar and butter with electric mixer in mixing bowl until light and fluffy. Add egg yolks; blend well. Add flour, nuts, and salt; blend well. Spread half of the dough in prepared pan. Carefully spread Apricot Filling over dough. Carefully spread remaining dough over filling. Bake 45 minutes, or until golden brown. Cool in pan before cutting into bars.

Apricot Filling

1/2 cup finely chopped dried
  apricots
1/2 cup water

1/3 cup sugar
1/2 teaspoon vanilla

Combine apricots and water in small saucepan. Cover and cook 20 minutes. Add sugar; cook, uncovered, until thick. Cool slightly. Stir in vanilla. Cool completely.

To make Strawberry Bars, substitute 1/2 cup strawberry jam for Apricot Filling.

Saucepan Brownies _____ 16 squares

1/2 cup butter or margarine
2 squares (1 ounce each)
  unsweetened chocolate
1 cup sugar
2 eggs

3/4 cup sifted Martha White
  Self-Rising Flour
1 teaspoon vanilla
3/4 cup chopped nuts

Preheat oven to 350°F. Grease 8-inch square baking pan; set aside. Melt butter and chocolate in saucepan over low heat. Remove from heat. Stir in remaining ingredients; mix well. Pour into prepared pan. Bake 30 minutes. Cool in pan on wire rack. Cut into 16 squares.

If using Martha White All-Purpose Flour, add 1/4 teaspoon salt and 1 1/2 teaspoons baking powder to flour.

Lemon Drop Cookies _____ 36 to 48 cookies

2 cups sifted Martha White
  Self-Rising Flour
1/4 teaspoon baking soda
1 cup sugar
1/2 cup vegetable shortening

1 egg
1 1/2 teaspoons grated lemon
  peel
2 tablespoons lemon juice
1 tablespoon water

Preheat oven to 375°F. Lightly grease 2 large baking sheets; set aside. Combine flour and baking soda in bowl; set aside. Cream sugar and shortening with electric mixer in large mixing bowl until light and fluffy. Add egg and lemon peel; blend well. Drop by teaspoonfuls onto prepared baking sheets. Bake 10 to 12 minutes, or until golden brown. Let stand 1 minute before transferring to wire racks to cool.

Holiday Fruit Bars _____ 24 bars

1 cup coarsely chopped nuts
3/4 cup sifted Martha White
  Self-Rising Flour,
  divided
1 cup chopped dates
3/4 cup mixed chopped
  candied fruit

2 eggs
1 cup confectioners sugar
1/3 cup butter or margarine,
  melted
Confectioners Sugar Glaze
(below)

Preheat oven to 325°F. Grease 9-inch square baking pan; set aside. Combine nuts, 1/2 cup flour, dates, and candied fruit in large bowl; set aside. Beat eggs with electric mixer in mixing bowl until thick and lemon-colored. Gradually beat in confectioners sugar. Blend in butter. Add remaining 1/4 cup flour; blend well. Stir in fruit mixture. Pour into prepared pan. Bake 35 minutes, or until toothpick inserted in center comes out clean. Spread with Confectioners Sugar Glaze while warm. Cool in pan on wire rack. Cut into bars.

Confectioners Sugar Glaze

1/2 cup confectioners sugar
2 1/2 teaspoons hot water

1/4 teaspoon almond extract

Combine all ingredients in small mixing bowl; beat with electric mixer until blended. Add more water if glaze is too thick.

95

Coconut Drop Cookies _____ 48 cookies

1/2 cup sugar
1/2 cup plus 2 tablespoons
firmly packed brown
sugar
1/2 cup butter or margarine
2 eggs

2 cups sifted Martha White
Self-Rising Flour
1/2 teaspoon vanilla
1 1/3 cups flaked coconut
1/2 cup chopped pecans

Preheat oven to 350°F. Lightly grease 2 large baking sheets; set aside. Cream sugars and butter with electric mixer in mixing bowl until light and fluffy. Add eggs, 1 at a time, beating well after each addition. Add flour and vanilla; blend well. Stir in coconut and pecans. Drop by tablespoonfuls onto prepared baking sheets. Bake 12 to 15 minutes, or until golden brown. Transfer to wire racks to cool.

Date Bars _____ 24 bars

3/4 cup chopped nuts
1/2 cup sifted Martha White
Self-Rising Flour
2 cups finely chopped dates

3 eggs
3/4 cup sugar
1 teaspoon vanilla
Confectioners sugar

Preheat oven to 350°F. Grease 9-inch square baking pan; set aside. Combine nuts, flour, and dates in small bowl; set aside. Beat eggs with electric mixer in large mixing bowl until thick and lemon-colored. Gradually beat in sugar. Add vanilla; blend well. Add date mixture; blend well. Pour into prepared pan; spread evenly. Bake 25 minutes, or until golden brown. Cut into bars while hot. Cool in pan on wire rack. Roll in or sprinkle with confectioners sugar.

What nuts do you have on hand? Pecans? Walnuts? Almonds? Any variety works fine for most cookies.

Butter Cookies _____ About 84 cookies

1/2 cup sugar	3 cups sifted Martha White
1 cup butter	All-Purpose Flour
1 egg	1/2 teaspoon baking powder
1 tablespoon vanilla	

Combine sugar, butter, and egg in mixing bowl; beat with electric mixer until smooth. Add vanilla; blend well. Sift in flour and baking powder; blend well. Cover and refrigerate about 1 hour. Preheat oven to 425°F. Roll out dough on lightly floured board or pastry cloth to 1/4 inch thickness. Cut out with decorative cookie cutters. Place on ungreased baking sheets. Bake 5 to 7 minutes, or until golden brown. Transfer to wire racks to cool.

Cooled cookies can be frosted with Confectioners Icing (page 44) and decorated as desired.

Peanut Butter Chocolate Kisses _____ 40 cookies

3/4 cup firmly packed brown sugar	1 teaspoon vanilla
1/2 cup chunky peanut butter	1 1/3 cups sifted Martha White Self-Rising Flour
1/3 cup butter or margarine	40 large milk chocolate
1 egg	kisses

Combine brown sugar, peanut butter, and butter in mixing bowl; beat with electric mixer until thoroughly blended. Add egg and vanilla; blend well. Add flour; blend well. Cover with aluminum foil. Refrigerate about 1 hour. Preheat oven to 375°F. Shape dough by tablespoonfuls into balls. Place on ungreased baking sheets. Bake 5 minutes. Remove baking sheets from oven. Press chocolate kiss into center of each cookie. Return to oven. Bake 3 minutes; watch carefully to avoid burning chocolate. Transfer to wire racks to cool. Cool completely before storing.

Thumbprints ⸺ About 96 cookies

1 recipe Butter Cookies
(page 97)

1/2 cup red jam or preserves,
such as strawberry,
raspberry, or cherry

Prepare Butter Cookie dough. Refrigerate about 1 hour. Preheat oven to 375°F. Shape dough into 1-inch balls. Place on ungreased baking sheets. Use finger or end of wooden spoon to make deep depression in center of each ball. Depression will open as cookies bake. Bake 10 minutes. Remove baking sheets from oven. Fill centers of cookies with 1/4 teaspoon jam. Return baking sheets to oven. Bake 5 minutes. Transfer to wire racks to cool.

Orange Oatmeal Cookies ⸺ About 48 cookies

2 cups sifted Martha White
Self-Rising Flour
2 cups sugar
1 teaspoon nutmeg
1 cup vegetable shortening

2 eggs, lightly beaten
1/4 cup grated orange peel
2 tablespoons orange juice
3 cups uncooked quick
oats

Preheat oven to 375°F. Lightly grease 2 large baking sheets; set aside. Sift flour, sugar, and nutmeg into large bowl. Add shortening, eggs, orange peel, and juice; blend well. Stir in oats. Drop by level tablespoonfuls 2 inches apart onto prepared baking sheets. Bake 12 to 14 minutes, or until lightly browned. Transfer to wire racks to cool.

It's a Piece of Cake

It wasn't easy selecting the recipes for this chapter because Martha White cakes are some of the finest to be found. So we chose to present our classic cake recipes — from glorious Gold Cake to magnificent Macaroon Cake — time-tested recipes requested by our loyal customers. From the first tempting piece to the last fought-over morsel, these cakes will please the most discriminating cake lovers.

Macaroon Cake _____ 1 cake

6 eggs, separated	1/2 teaspoon coconut extract
1 cup vegetable shortening	3 cups sifted Martha White
1/2 cup butter or margarine	All-Purpose Flour
3 cups sugar	1 cup milk
1/4 teaspoon salt	2 2/3 cups flaked coconut
1/2 teaspoon almond extract	

Preheat oven to 300°F. Grease and flour 10-inch tube pan; set aside. Place egg whites in large mixing bowl. Beat at high speed of electric mixer until soft peaks form; set aside. Combine egg yolks, shortening, and butter in separate mixing bowl; beat until well blended. Gradually beat in sugar and salt; beat until light and fluffy. Beat in extracts. Alternately beat in flour and milk, beginning and ending with flour. Add coconut; blend well. Gently fold in egg whites with rubber spatula until blended. Pour into prepared pan. Bake 2 hours, or until toothpick inserted in center comes out clean. Cool in pan 15 minutes. Gently loosen sides of cake from pan. Turn out onto wire rack to cool completely. Decorate with toasted coconut and confectioners sugar before serving, if desired.

Aunt E. C.'s Pound Cake _____ 1 cake

1 pound (3 1/2 cups) sugar	1 pound (4 cups) sifted
1 pound (2 cups) butter	Martha White
1 pound (10 large or 12	All-Purpose Flour
small) eggs	

Generously grease 10-inch tube pan; set aside. Preheat oven to 300°F. Cream sugar and butter with electric mixer in mixing bowl until light and fluffy. Add eggs, 1 at a time, beating well after each addition. Gradually beat in flour; blend well. Pour into prepared pan. Bake 2 hours, or until toothpick inserted in center comes out clean. Cool in pans 10 minutes. Turn out onto wire rack to cool completely.

For an extra special serving touch, top with sweetened whipped cream and sliced bananas.

Macaroon Cake →

Texas Fruitcake _____ 1 cake

4 1/4 cups sifted Martha White
All-Purpose Flour,
divided
2 teaspoons baking powder
1/2 teaspoon salt
1 1/2 cups broken pecans
1 pound candied cherries,
halved

2 2/3 cups flaked coconut
2 cups sugar
1 1/2 cups butter, softened;
do not use substitute
6 eggs
1/2 cup orange juice

Preheat oven to 225°F. Grease and flour 10-inch tube pan; set aside. Combine 4 cups flour, baking powder, and salt in bowl; set aside. Combine pecans, cherries, coconut, and remaining 1/4 cup flour in small bowl; toss lightly to coat; set aside. Cream sugar and butter with electric mixer in mixing bowl until light and fluffy. Add eggs, 1 at a time, beating well after each addition. Alternately beat in flour mixture and orange juice, beginning and ending with flour mixture. Add fruit-nut mixture; blend well. Pour into prepared pan. Bake 4 hours, or until light brown and cake shrinks away slightly from sides of pan. Cool in pan on wire rack.

For better flavor and easy slicing, wrap fruitcake in aluminum foil and store in refrigerator several days before serving.

Carrot Pineapple Nut Cake _____ 1 cake

2 cups sifted Martha White
Self-Rising Flour
2 teaspoons cinnamon
2 cups sugar
1 1/2 cups vegetable oil

4 eggs
2 cups finely grated carrots
1 can (8 1/4 ounces) crushed
pineapple, undrained
3/4 cup chopped nuts

Preheat oven to 325°F. Grease and flour 15 × 10 × 2-inch pan; set aside. Combine flour and cinnamon in bowl; set aside. Combine sugar, oil, and eggs in large mixing bowl; beat with electric mixer until well blended. Gradually beat in flour mixture; blend well. Stir in carrots, pineapple, and nuts. Pour into prepared pan. Bake 55 to 60 minutes, or until cake shrinks slightly away from sides of pan. Cool in pan 10 minutes. Turn out onto wire rack to cool completely. Frost with half a recipe Cream Cheese Icing (page 107).

Fresh Coconut Cake _____ 1 cake

5 egg whites (2/3 cup)
1 1/2 cups sugar
3/4 cup vegetable shortening
1 teaspoon vanilla
2 1/2 cups sifted Martha White
    Self-Rising Flour

1 cup milk
1 fresh coconut
White Cloud Icing
    (page 111)

Preheat oven to 375°F. Grease and flour two 8-inch square or 9-inch round baking pans; set aside. Place egg whites in small mixing bowl. Beat at high speed of electric mixer until stiff peaks form; set aside. Cream sugar and shortening with electric mixer in mixing bowl until light and fluffy, scraping bowl with rubber spatula. Beat in vanilla. Alternately beat in flour and milk, beginning and ending with flour. Gently fold in egg whites. Pour into prepared pans. Bake 25 to 30 minutes, or until toothpick inserted in centers comes out clean. Cool in pans 10 minutes. Turn out onto wire racks to cool completely. Drain milk from coconut (about 1/3 cup); reserve. Grate coconut; set aside. Place bottom cake layer on serving plate. Sprinkle half of the coconut milk over top. Sprinkle remaining coconut milk over second layer. Frost bottom layer with White Cloud Icing. Add top layer. Frost top and sides with White Cloud Icing. Sprinkle top and sides with grated coconut. Store cake in refrigerator. For best results, store 1 day before serving.

To drain coconut, pierce "eyes" with sharp pick and hammer. Pour out liquid. Refrigerate until ready to use; up to 24 hours.

To grate coconut, separate meat from shell. Use a vegetable peeler to remove skin. Cut meat into chunks. Grate or chop in blender or food processor.

How Much Does It Yield?

☐ 8- or 9-inch layer cake   = 10 to 16 servings
☐ 8- or 9-inch round or square cake = 9 servings
☐ 13 × 9 × 2-inch sheet cake   = 12 to 15 servings
☐ 10 × 4-inch tube cake   = 12 to 16 servings
☐ 15 × 10-inch sheet cake   = 14 to 16 servings

First Prize Chocolate Cake ———————— 1 cake

1/2 cup butter or margarine
4 squares (1 ounce each)
  unsweetened chocolate
2 eggs
2 cups buttermilk
2 teaspoons vanilla

2 1/2 cups sifted Martha White
  Self-Rising Flour
2 cups sugar
1 teaspoon baking soda
Dark Chocolate Frosting
  (below)

Preheat oven to 350°F. Grease and flour two 9-inch round or 8-inch square baking pans; set aside. Combine butter and chocolate in top of double boiler or saucepan. Place over low heat until chocolate melts, stirring constantly. Break eggs into large mixing bowl; beat with electric mixer 2 minutes, or until frothy. Add buttermilk and vanilla; blend well. Sift flour, sugar, and baking soda into separate bowl. Stir flour mixture into buttermilk mixture. Add melted butter and chocolate; blend well. Pour into prepared pans. Bake 30 minutes, or until toothpick inserted in centers comes out clean. Cool in pans 10 minutes. Turn out onto wire racks to cool completely. Frost with Dark Chocolate Frosting.

Dark Chocolate Frosting ———————— About 3 cups

1/2 cup butter or margarine
4 squares (1 ounce each)
  unsweetened chocolate
4 1/2 cups (16 ounces)
  confectioners sugar,
  sifted

1/4 teaspoon salt
1/2 cup evaporated milk,
  undiluted
2 teaspoons vanilla

Combine butter and chocolate in top of double boiler or saucepan. Place over low heat until chocolate melts, stirring constantly. Gradually stir in confectioners sugar. Add salt, milk, and vanilla; beat with electric mixer until smooth.

Orange Cake _____ 1 cake

1 1/4 cups sugar
1/2 cup vegetable shortening
1/4 cup butter or margarine
8 egg yolks
2 cups sifted Martha White
Self-Rising Flour

3/4 cup buttermilk
1 teaspoon vanilla
1/2 teaspoon orange extract
Orange Filling (below)
Orange Cream Cheese Icing
(below)

Preheat oven to 350°F. Grease and flour two 9-inch round or 8-inch square baking pans; set aside. Cream sugar, shortening, and butter with electric mixer in mixing bowl until light and fluffy. Beat in egg yolks, 1 at a time, beating well after each addition. Alternately beat in flour and buttermilk, beginning and ending with flour, just until blended. Add vanilla and orange extract; blend well. Pour into prepared pans. Bake 30 minutes, or until toothpick inserted in centers comes out clean. Cool in pans 10 minutes. Turn out onto wire racks to cool completely. Place bottom layer on cake plate. Spread Orange Filling evenly over layer. Add top layer. Frost cake with Orange Cream Cheese Icing.

Orange Filling

3/4 cup sugar
3 tablespoons cornstarch
1/4 teaspoon salt
2/3 cup water

1/2 cup orange juice
1 tablespoon grated orange
peel
2 tablespoons butter

Combine sugar, cornstarch, and salt in saucepan. Stir in water, orange juice, and orange peel. Bring mixture to a boil, stirring constantly. Boil about 1 minute. Remove from heat. Stir in butter. Chill before filling cake.

Orange Cream Cheese Icing

2 packages (3 ounces each)
cream cheese, at room
temperature
1/4 cup butter or margarine
4 1/2 cups (16 ounces)
confectioners sugar,
sifted

1 teaspoon grated orange
peel
1/2 teaspoon orange extract

Combine cream cheese and butter in small mixing bowl; blend thoroughly with electric mixer. Gradually beat in confectioners sugar. Add orange peel and extract; beat until smooth and creamy.

Yellow Layer Cake _____ 1 cake

2 cups sifted Martha White
    Self-Rising Flour
1 1/2 cups sugar
1 cup buttermilk
3 eggs

1/3 cup vegetable shortening
1/3 cup butter or margarine
1 teaspoon vanilla
Real Fudge Frosting
    (below)

Preheat oven to 350°F. Grease and flour two 9-inch round or 8-inch square baking pans; set aside. Combine all ingredients, except frosting, in large mixing bowl. Beat at low speed of electric mixer 30 seconds, or just until blended, scraping bowl constantly. Beat at high speed 3 minutes, scraping bowl occasionally. Pour into prepared pans. Bake 30 minutes, or until toothpick inserted in centers comes out clean. Cool in pans 10 minutes. Turn out onto wire racks to cool completely. Frost with Real Fudge Frosting.

For a more open-textured cake, substitute 7/8 cup whole milk for 1 cup buttermilk.

Real Fudge Frosting _____ About 3 cups

2 squares (1 ounce each)
    unsweetened chocolate
1/2 cup heavy cream
1/4 cup milk
2 cups sugar

Pinch salt
1 tablespoon corn syrup
1 tablespoon butter or
    margarine
1 teaspoon vanilla

Combine chocolate, cream, and milk in saucepan. Cook over low heat, stirring constantly, until chocolate melts. Add sugar, salt, and corn syrup. Bring to a boil over moderate heat, stirring constantly, until soft-ball stage (232°F on candy thermometer; drop of mixture forms a soft ball when dropped in cold water). Remove from heat. Add butter and vanilla. Let stand 15 minutes. Beat with electric mixer until spreading consistency. If frosting becomes too thick, beat in small amount additional heavy cream.

Gold Cake _____ 1 cake

2 1/2 cups sifted Martha White
    Self-Rising Flour
1 2/3 cups sugar
1/2 cup vegetable shortening

1 1/4 cups milk, divided
1 1/2 teaspoons vanilla
5 egg yolks
Caramel Icing (below)

Preheat oven to 350°F. Grease and lightly flour two 9-inch round or 8-inch square baking pans; set aside. Sift flour and sugar into large mixing bowl. Add shortening and a little more than half of the milk; beat 2 minutes with electric mixer. Add remaining milk, vanilla, and egg yolks; beat 2 minutes. Pour into prepared pans. Bake 30 minutes, or until toothpick inserted in centers comes out clean. Cool in pans 10 minutes. Turn out onto wire racks to cool completely. Frost with Caramel Icing.

Caramel Icing _____ About 4 cups

2 1/2 cups sugar, divided
1 cup milk

1/4 cup butter or margarine
1 teaspoon vanilla

Combine 2 cups sugar and milk in heavy saucepan. Bring to a boil over moderate heat until soft-ball stage (232°F on candy thermometer; drop of mixture forms a soft ball when dropped in cold water). Remove from heat; set aside. Place remaining 1/2 cup sugar in heavy skillet. Cook over moderate heat, stirring constantly, until golden brown and caramelized. Stir into milk mixture. Add butter and vanilla; beat at high speed of electric mixer 5 minutes. Mixture will thicken as it cools.

Cream Cheese Icing _____ 3 cups

1 package (8 ounces) cream
    cheese, at room
    temperature
1/2 cup butter or margarine,
    softened

4 1/2 cups (16 ounces)
    confectioners sugar,
    sifted
2 teaspoons vanilla

Combine all ingredients in mixing bowl. Beat with electric mixer until smooth and creamy.

This recipe frosts 8- or 9-inch layer cake or 13 × 9 × 2-inch sheet cake. For smaller cake, cut recipe in half.

Pineapple Pecan Upside-Down Cake _____ 1 cake

4 tablespoons butter or margarine	1 1/2 cups sifted Martha White Self-Rising Flour
1/2 cup firmly packed brown sugar	1 cup sugar
6 slices canned pineapple, in heavy syrup, drained; reserve syrup	1/2 cup vegetable shortening
6 maraschino cherries	1 egg, lightly beaten
35 pecan halves	1 teaspoon vanilla

Preheat oven to 350°F. Melt butter in 10-inch cake pan or iron skillet in oven. Dissolve brown sugar in 1 tablespoon reserved pineapple syrup in small dish. Spread evenly in baking pan. Arrange pineapple slices in bottom of pan. Place pecans, rounded sides down, in and around pineapple; set aside. Pour remaining reserved pineapple syrup into measuring cup; add enough water to measure 1/2 cup; pour into large mixing bowl. Add flour, sugar, shortening, egg, and vanilla. Beat at low speed of electric mixer 2 minutes, or until well blended. Spoon over pineapple and pecans. Bake 35 to 40 minutes, or until toothpick inserted in center comes out clean. Cool in pan 5 minutes. Turn out onto large serving plate. Garnish with cherries. Serve warm, topped with sweetened whipped cream, if desired.

Fresh Apple Nut Cake _____ 1 cake

2 eggs	3 cups chopped peeled apples
1 3/4 cups sugar	1 teaspoon cinnamon
1 cup vegetable oil	1 teaspoon vanilla
2 1/2 cups sifted Martha White Self-Rising Flour	Cream Cheese Icing (page 107)
1 cup chopped walnuts	

Preheat oven to 300°F. Grease 13 × 9 × 2-inch baking pan; set aside. Combine eggs, sugar, and oil in bowl; blend well. Gradually add flour; blend well. Stir in walnuts, apples, cinnamon, and vanilla; blend well. Pour into prepared pan. Bake 1 hour 10 minutes, or until toothpick inserted in center comes out clean. Cool in pan. Frost with Cream Cheese Icing.

← Pineapple Pecan Upside-Down Cake

Jelly Roll _____ 10 servings

3 large eggs
1 cup sugar
1/4 cup water
1 teaspoon vanilla
1 cup sifted Martha White
Self-Rising Flour

Confectioners sugar
1 cup red jelly or jam, such
as strawberry,
raspberry, or cherry

Preheat oven to 375°F. Grease and flour 15 × 10 × 1-inch jelly-roll pan; set aside. Break eggs into small mixing bowl; beat with electric mixer until thick and lemon-colored. Gradually beat in sugar. Add water and vanilla; blend well. Gradually beat in flour until smooth. Pour into prepared pan. Bake 12 minutes, or until golden brown. Remove from oven; loosen edges with sharp knife. Immediately turn out onto tea towel sprinkled with confectioners sugar. Trim any stiff edges. Spread jelly over cake. Carefully roll up, jelly-roll fashion, from narrow end, using towel to ease cake over. Cool, wrapped in towel, on wire rack about 1/2 hour. Carefully remove towel. Sprinkle confectioners sugar over top, if desired. Slice to serve.

German Chocolate Cake _____ 1 cake

1 bar (4 ounces) German
sweet chocolate
1/2 cup hot water
2 cups sugar
1 cup butter or margarine
4 eggs

2 1/2 cups sifted Martha White
Self-Rising Flour
1 cup milk
1 teaspoon vanilla
German Coconut Topping
(page 111)

Preheat oven to 350°F. Grease and flour bottom of one 15 × 10 × 2-inch or three 9-inch round baking pans; set aside. Combine chocolate and water in small bowl; stir to melt chocolate; set aside to cool. Cream sugar and butter with electric mixer in mixing bowl until light and fluffy. Add eggs, 1 at a time, beating well after each addition. Alternately beat in flour and milk, beginning and ending with flour. Add chocolate mixture and vanilla; blend well. Pour into prepared pans. Bake 45 minutes, or until toothpick inserted in centers comes out clean. Cool in pans 10 minutes. Turn onto serving plate. Frost with German Coconut Topping. (Frost middle and top layer, if making layer cake.)

German Coconut Topping _____ About 5 cups

1 cup sugar	3 egg yolks
1 cup evaporated milk, undiluted	1 1/3 cups flaked coconut
1/2 cup butter or margarine	1 cup chopped pecans
	1 teaspoon vanilla

Combine sugar, milk, butter, and egg yolks in saucepan. Cook over moderate heat, stirring constantly, 12 minutes, or until thickened. Stir in coconut, pecans, and vanilla. Beat with electric mixer until thick enough to spread.

Rich White Cake _____ 1 cake

2 1/2 cups sifted Martha White Self-Rising Flour	1 cup milk, divided
1 1/2 cups sugar	1 1/2 teaspoons vanilla
3/4 cup vegetable shortening	5 egg whites
	White Cloud Icing (below)

Preheat oven to 350°F. Grease and flour two 9-inch round baking pans; set aside. Sift flour and sugar into mixing bowl. Add shortening, 3/4 cup milk, and vanilla; beat at low speed of electric mixer just until blended. Beat at medium speed 2 minutes. Add egg whites and remaining 1/4 cup milk. Beat at medium speed 2 minutes. Pour into prepared pans. Bake 30 to 35 minutes, or until toothpick inserted in centers comes out clean. Cool in pans 10 minutes. Turn out onto wire racks to cool completely. Frost with White Cloud Icing.

White Cloud Icing _____ About 3 cups

1 1/2 cups sugar	Dash salt
1/3 cup water	3 egg whites
1/4 teaspoon cream of tartar	1 teaspoon vanilla

Combine sugar, water, cream of tartar, and salt in saucepan. Bring to a boil over moderate heat, stirring constantly. Reduce heat; cover and simmer 3 minutes. Remove cover. Bring to a boil; boil to soft-ball stage (232°F on candy thermometer; drop of mixture forms a soft ball when dropped in cold water). Remove from heat. Beat egg whites with electric mixer in mixing bowl until stiff but not dry. Continue to beat while slowly adding syrup. Add vanilla. Beat until stiff peaks form.

Boston Cream Pie _____ 1 cake

2 cups sifted Martha White Self-Rising Flour	1/3 cup butter or margarine
1 1/2 cups sugar	3 eggs
1 cup buttermilk	1 teaspoon vanilla
1/3 cup vegetable shortening	Cream Filling (below)
	Chocolate Glaze (below)

Preheat oven to 350°F. Grease and flour two 9-inch round baking pans; set aside. Combine all ingredients except Cream Filling and Chocolate Glaze in large mixing bowl. Beat at low speed of electric mixer 30 seconds, scraping bowl often. Beat at high speed 3 minutes. Pour into prepared pans. Bake 30 minutes, or until toothpick inserted in centers comes out clean. Cool in pans 10 minutes. Turn out of pans onto wire racks to cool completely. Place bottom layer on cake plate. Spread Cream Filling evenly over layer. Add top layer. Drizzle warm Chocolate Glaze over top of cake.

Cream Filling

1/2 cup sugar	2 eggs, lightly beaten
1/3 cup sifted Martha White Self-Rising Flour	2 cups hot milk
	1 1/2 teaspoons vanilla

Combine sugar and flour in top of double boiler; gradually stir in eggs and hot milk. Cook over simmering water 20 minutes, stirring occasionally. Remove from heat; stir in vanilla. Cover with plastic wrap. Chill thoroughly before filling cake.

Chocolate Glaze

1/2 cup sugar	1/2 cup sifted confectioners sugar
1/4 cup cocoa	
3 tablespoons water	
2 tablespoons butter or margarine	

Combine sugar, cocoa, water, and butter in saucepan. Cook over low heat, stirring constantly, until mixture comes to a boil. Remove from heat. Gradually stir in confectioners sugar until smooth.

You're So Sweet

Make the end of the meal more than just dessert by serving any of the satisfying treats featured in this chapter. Make your special after-dinner presentation the richly delicious Chess Cake or Caramel Dumplings. The overwhelming reaction will be the smiles you receive and the voices that say, "Thank you. You're so sweet."

Chocolate Eclairs _____ 14 eclairs

1 recipe Cream Puffs
(page 119)

French Custard (below)
Chocolate Glaze (below)

Preheat oven to 375°F. Grease 2 baking sheets; set aside. Prepare Cream Puff dough. Press dough through pastry bag with no tip, or use spoon to shape 4 × 1-inch logs on prepared baking sheets. Bake 30 to 35 minutes, or until golden brown and eclairs sound hollow when lightly tapped with fingertips. Immediately pierce each with tip of fork to allow steam to escape. Return to oven 5 to 7 minutes to dry out. Transfer to wire racks to cool completely. Slice off tops. Fill with French Custard. Replace tops. Place eclairs on wire rack. Pour warm Chocolate Glaze over tops.

French Custard

1/3 cup sugar
1 tablespoon Martha White
All-Purpose Flour
1 tablespoon cornstarch
1/4 teaspoon salt

1 1/2 cups milk
1 egg yolk, lightly beaten
1 teaspoon vanilla
1/2 cup heavy cream, whipped

Combine sugar, flour, cornstarch, and salt in saucepan. Gradually stir in milk. Bring to a boil over moderate heat, stirring until thick. Reduce heat to low. Cook, stirring constantly, 2 to 3 minutes. Stir small amount custard into egg yolk. Return all to saucepan. Cook and stir until custard just comes to a boil. Remove from heat. Stir in vanilla; let stand until cool. Beat with electric mixer until smooth. Fold in whipped cream until well blended.

Chocolate Glaze

1 package (6 ounces) semisweet chocolate pieces
2 tablespoons butter or
margarine

3 tablespoons milk
2 tablespoons light corn
syrup

Melt chocolate and butter in heavy saucepan over low heat, stirring constantly. Add milk and corn syrup. Stir until smooth. Remove from heat. Let stand to cool slightly.

Country Kitchen Gingerbread _____ 12 to 16 servings

2 cups sifted Martha White
   Self-Rising Flour
1/4 teaspoon baking soda
1 teaspoon cinnamon
1 teaspoon ginger
1/2 teaspoon ground cloves
1/2 cup firmly packed brown
   sugar

1/2 cup vegetable shortening
2 eggs
3/4 cup molasses
1 cup hot water
Nut Topping (below)

Preheat oven to 350°F. Grease 13 × 9 × 2-inch baking pan; set aside. Combine flour, baking soda, and spices in small bowl; set aside. Cream brown sugar and shortening with electric mixer in mixing bowl until light and fluffy. Add eggs and molasses; blend well. Alternately beat in flour mixture and hot water, beginning and ending with flour mixture. Pour into prepared pan. Sprinkle Nut Topping over cake. Bake 35 minutes, or until toothpick inserted in center comes out clean.

Nut Topping

1/2 cup firmly packed brown
   sugar
1/2 cup chopped nuts
1/4 cup Martha White
   All-Purpose Flour

1 1/2 teaspoons cinnamon
1/4 cup butter or margarine,
   softened

Combine all ingredients in small bowl; blend well.

Bishop's Bread _____ 1 loaf

2 cups chopped walnuts
1 1/2 cups sifted Martha White
   Self-Rising Flour
2/3 cup semisweet chocolate
   pieces

1 cup finely chopped dates
1 cup candied cherries,
   cut in half
3 eggs
3/4 cup sugar

Preheat oven to 325°F. Grease 9 × 5 × 3-inch loaf pan; set aside. Combine walnuts, flour, chocolate, dates, and cherries in bowl. Break eggs into large mixing bowl; beat with electric mixer until lemon-colored. Gradually beat in sugar until well blended. Stir in flour mixture; blend well. Pour into prepared pan. Bake 1 hour 20 minutes, or until toothpick inserted in center comes out clean. Cool in pan on wire rack.

Strawberry Shortcake ——— 8 to 10 servings

2 cups sifted Martha White
　　Self-Rising Flour
3 tablespoons sugar
1/3 cup butter or margarine
1 egg

About 1/2 cup milk
3 to 4 cups sliced strawberries,
　　sweetened with sugar
　　to taste
1/2 pint heavy cream, whipped

Preheat oven to 450°F. Grease large baking sheet; set aside. Combine flour and sugar in mixing bowl. Cut in butter with pastry blender or 2 knives until mixture is consistency of coarse crumbs. Beat egg with fork in measuring cup. Add enough milk to measure 2/3 cup. Add to flour mixture; stir with fork until dough leaves sides of bowl. Turn out onto lightly floured board or pastry cloth. Knead 3 or 4 times, or until smooth. Roll dough out to 1/2-inch thickness. Cut into rounds with floured 2 1/2-inch biscuit cutter. Place on prepared baking sheet. Bake 10 to 12 minutes, or until golden brown. Transfer to wire rack to cool 5 minutes. Split shortcake in half crosswise. Spoon sweetened strawberries and whipped cream onto bottom halves. Replace tops. Top with remaining strawberries and whipped cream.

To make 1 large shortcake, pat dough into greased 8-inch round baking pan. Bake 15 to 18 minutes. Transfer to wire rack to cool 5 minutes before splitting and filling.

Apple Good ——————————————— 6 servings

1 cup sugar
3/4 cup plus 1 tablespoon
　　Martha White All-Purpose
　　Flour, sifted, divided
1/2 teaspoon cinnamon
1/2 cup chopped nuts (optional)
3 cups chopped peeled apples

3/4 cup uncooked quick oats
3/4 cup firmly packed brown
　　sugar
1/2 cup butter or margarine,
　　melted

Preheat oven to 350°F. Grease and lightly flour 9-inch square baking pan; set aside. Combine sugar, 1 tablespoon flour, cinnamon, and nuts in small bowl; toss lightly to mix. Place apples in separate bowl; sprinkle with sugar mixture; toss lightly to mix. Place in prepared pan. Combine oats, remaining 3/4 cup flour, brown sugar, and butter in small bowl; toss lightly to mix. Sprinkle over apples. Press mixture lightly into apples. Bake 30 minutes, or until golden brown.

Strawberry Shortcake →

Cherry Turnovers ———————— 18 turnovers

2 cups sifted Martha White
  Self-Rising Flour
2/3 cup butter or margarine,
  softened

1 egg, lightly beaten
1/4 cup cold water
1 can (21 ounces) cherry
  pie filling

Place flour in bowl. Cut in butter with pastry blender or 2 knives until mixture is consistency of coarse crumbs. Add egg and water; stir with fork until mixture leaves sides of bowl. Shape into ball; divide in half. Roll out each half on lightly floured board or pastry cloth into 1/8-inch thick rectangle. Use sharp knife or pizza cutter to cut out eighteen 4-inch squares. Place 6 squares on ungreased baking sheet. Place in refrigerator. Repeat for remaining 12 squares on 2 additional baking sheets. Working with one baking sheet at a time, spoon 1 heaping tablespoon pie filling onto 1 corner of each square. Fold opposite corner over to form triangle. Use floured fork to press edges together. Prick tops with fork. Return to refrigerator. Remove baking sheets from refrigerator. Preheat oven to 400°F. Bake 15 to 18 minutes, or until golden brown. Transfer to wire racks to cool. Heat remaining filling. Spoon over warm turnovers to serve.

Other prepared pie fillings can be used, such as blueberry, strawberry, apple, or blackberry.

Pumpkin Cupcakes ———————— 18 cupcakes

1 1/2 cups sifted Martha White
  Self-Rising Flour
1 teaspoon cinnamon
1 cup sugar
3/4 cup canned pumpkin
1/2 cup plus 2 tablespoons
  vegetable oil

2 eggs
1/2 cup seedless golden
  raisins
1/2 cup chopped pecans

Preheat oven to 350°F. Grease or paper line 18 muffin cups; set aside. Combine flour and cinnamon in small bowl; set aside. Combine sugar, pumpkin, and oil in mixing bowl; beat with electric mixer until blended. Add eggs, 1 at a time, beating well after each addition. Add flour mixture; blend well. Stir in raisins and pecans. Fill muffin cups two-thirds full. Bake 20 to 25 minutes, or until toothpick inserted in centers comes out clean. Transfer to wire racks to cool. Frost with half recipe Cream Cheese Icing (page 107)

Cream Puffs _____ 10 regular-size puffs

1 cup water
1/2 cup butter or margarine
1 cup sifted Martha White
  Self-Rising Flour

4 eggs, at room
  temperature
French Custard (page 114)

Grease large baking sheet; set aside. Combine water and butter in saucepan; bring to a full boil over moderate heat. Reduce heat to low. While stirring vigorously, add flour all at once. Stir constantly over low heat until mixture pulls away from pan and forms a ball. Remove from heat. Add eggs, 1 at a time, beating well after each addition. (Electric mixer can be used.) Beat until shiny and smooth. Preheat oven to 375°F. For miniature cream puffs, drop batter by teaspoonfuls, 2 inches apart, onto prepared baking sheet. For regular cream puffs, drop batter by tablespoonfuls, 3 inches apart, onto prepared baking sheet. Bake miniature puffs 25 to 30 minutes, regular puffs 35 to 40 minutes, or until golden brown and puffs sound hollow when lightly tapped with fingertips. Remove from oven. Immediately pierce each with tip of knife to allow steam to escape. Return to oven 5 to 7 minutes to dry out. Transfer to wire rack to cool completely. Slice off tops. Fill with French Custard or desired filling. Replace tops.

Chess Cake _____ 1 cake

1 cup butter or margarine
1 box (16 ounces) light
  brown sugar
3/4 cup sugar
1 1/2 teaspoons vanilla

4 eggs
2 cups sifted Martha White
  Self-Rising Flour
1 cup broken nuts (optional)
Confectioners sugar

Preheat oven to 350°F. Grease and flour 13 × 9 × 2-inch baking pan; set aside. Melt butter in large saucepan over low heat. Remove from heat. Add sugars and vanilla; blend well. Add eggs, 1 at a time, beating well after each addition. Add flour; blend well. Stir in nuts. Pour into prepared pan. Bake 40 minutes. Turn out onto wire rack. Sprinkle confectioners sugar over top. Let stand until cool. Cut into squares.

This cake has a pudding-like consistency and will fall slightly after it is removed from oven.

Superfast Blackberry Cobbler _____ 6 to 8 servings

1/2 cup butter or margarine	1 cup sifted Martha White
1 can (16 ounces) black-	Self-Rising Flour
berries with juice	3/4 cup sugar
(about 2 cups)	3/4 cup milk

Preheat oven to 350°F. Melt butter in 8-inch square baking pan in oven. Place blackberries and juice in small saucepan; place over low heat until heated through. Combine flour, sugar, and milk in bowl; blend well. Pour into baking pan with melted butter; do not stir. Spoon blackberries and juice evenly over batter; do not stir. Bake 40 to 45 minutes, or until golden brown. Serve warm with cream, if desired.

Pitted cherries or sliced peaches can be substituted for blackberries. Add 1/4 cup sugar to unsweetened fruit.

Trifle _____ 6 to 8 servings

1 layer Yellow Layer Cake	6 tablespoons slivered
(page 106)	almonds, toasted,
1/4 cup orange juice	divided
1/2 cup raspberry or	1/2 pint (1 cup) heavy
strawberry jam	cream
Boiled Custard (page 121),	1 tablespoon sugar
chilled	

Split cake crosswise in half. Sprinkle each half with half of the orange juice. Spread each with half of the jam. Place 1 half in bottom of 8- or 9-inch serving bowl. Spoon half of the Boiled Custard over top. Sprinkle with 2 tablespoons almonds. Top with remaining cake, custard, and 2 tablespoons almonds. Cover and refrigerate 3 to 4 hours. Beat cream at high speed of electric mixer in mixing bowl, gradually adding sugar, until stiff peaks form. To serve, spoon sweetened whipped cream over top of Trifle. Sprinkle with remaining 2 tablespoons almonds. Serve directly from bowl.

Boiled Custard

3 cups milk
1 stick cinnamon (optional)
5 egg yolks, lightly beaten

5 tablespoons sugar
1/4 teaspoon salt
1 teaspoon vanilla

Combine milk and cinnamon in top of double boiler. Heat until tiny bubbles appear around edge. Combine egg yolks, sugar, and salt in bowl; blend well. Slowly add hot milk mixture, stirring constantly. Return mixture to double boiler. Cook over hot, not boiling, water, stirring constantly, until custard coats back of spoon. Discard cinnamon. Immediately pour into chilled pitcher or bowl. Stir in vanilla. Chill thoroughly before using.

Danish Pudding Cake _____ 1 cake

2 cups sugar
1 cup butter or margarine
4 eggs
1 teaspoon vanilla
3 cups sifted Martha White
    All-Purpose Flour
1/2 teaspoon salt

1/2 teaspoon baking powder
1/2 cup milk
1 package (8 ounces) chopped
    dates
1 cup chopped pecans
Orange Sauce (below)

Preheat oven to 325°F. Grease and flour 10-inch tube pan; set aside. Cream sugar and butter with electric mixer in large mixing bowl until light and fluffy. Add eggs, 1 at a time, beating well after each addition; stir in vanilla. Combine flour, salt, and baking powder in separate bowl. Alternately add flour mixture and milk to creamed mixture; blend well. Stir in dates and pecans. Pour into prepared pan. Bake 1 hour 15 minutes, or until toothpick inserted in center comes out clean. While cake is baking, prepare Orange Sauce. Remove cake from oven; immediately spoon sauce over top. Cool completely in pan.

Orange Sauce

1 cup sugar
1 cup orange juice

2 tablespoons grated orange
    peel

Combine all ingredients in small saucepan. Bring to a boil, stirring constantly. Remove from heat; cool slightly.

121

Mom's Apple Cobbler _____ 8 servings

1/2 cup butter or margarine	1/2 cup vegetable shortening
2 cups sugar	1/3 cup milk
2 cups water	2 cups finely chopped peeled
1 1/2 cups sifted Martha White	apples
Self-Rising Flour	1 teaspoon cinnamon

Preheat oven to 350°F. Melt butter in 13 × 9 × 2-inch baking pan. Remove from oven; set aside. Combine sugar and water in saucepan; cook over moderate heat until sugar dissolves. Remove from heat; set aside. Place flour in bowl. Cut in shortening with pastry blender or 2 knives until mixture is consistency of coarse crumbs. Add milk; stir with fork just until dough leaves sides of bowl. Turn out onto lightly floured board or pastry cloth. Knead just until smooth. Roll out into 1/4-inch thick rectangle. Place apples in small bowl. Sprinkle cinnamon over apples; toss lightly to mix. Spread apples evenly over dough. Roll up, jelly-roll fashion, from long side. Moisten edge with water; pinch to seal. Cut into 1/2-inch thick slices. Place slices, cut sides down, over butter in baking pan. Pour sugar syrup over top. Bake 1 hour.

Fresh, frozen, or canned fruit can be substituted for apples. If packed in liquid, drain and reserve liquid for use in sugar syrup, adding water to measure 2 cups.

Coconut Cream Stack Pie _____ 8 servings

Pastry for 2-crust pie	1/4 teaspoon salt
(page 76); omit salt	1 cup milk
3/4 cup plus 2 tablespoons	1 cup half-and-half
sugar	3 eggs, separated
3 tablespoons Martha White	1 teaspoon vanilla
Self-Rising Flour	1/2 cup flaked coconut
1 tablespoon cornstarch	1/4 teaspoon cream of tartar

Preheat oven to 450°F. Roll out dough on lightly floured board or pastry cloth to 1/4 inch thickness. Using 8-inch cake pan as guide, cut into four 8-inch circles. Transfer to baking sheet. Prick well with fork. Bake 8 to 10 minutes, or until lightly browned. Use wide spatula to transfer to wire rack to cool. Combine 1/2 cup sugar, flour, cornstarch, and salt in small bowl; set aside. Combine milk and half-and-half in saucepan; bring to a simmer but do not boil. Stir sugar mixture into milk mixture. Cook over low heat, stirring constantly, until custard is very thick. Remove from heat. Place egg yolks in small bowl; beat lightly with fork. Stir small amount of custard into egg yolks. Return all to saucepan. Cook, stirring constantly, about 2 minutes. Remove from heat. Stir in vanilla and coconut; set aside. Place egg whites and cream of tartar in mixing bowl. Beat with electric mixer, adding remaining sugar, a little at a time, until stiff peaks form; set aside. Place 1 pastry circle on 10-inch circle of aluminum foil on baking sheet. Spoon 1/2 cup custard over circle to 1/4 inch of edge. Top with another pastry circle and 1/2 cup custard. Repeat with remaining pastry, ending with custard. Spread meringue over top and sides of stack. Preheat oven to 400°F. Bake 8 to 10 minutes, or until peaks are golden brown. Transfer to wire rack to cool, away from draft. Cut into 8 wedges to serve.

Caramel Dumplings ———— 6 to 8 servings

1 1/2 cups sugar, divided
1 1/4 cups boiling water
2 tablespoons butter, divided
Dash salt
1 teaspoon vanilla, divided
1 cup sifted Martha White Self-Rising Flour
1/4 cup milk

Heat 1/4 cup sugar in heavy, ovenproof skillet over moderate heat, stirring constantly, until golden brown and caramelized. Gradually stir in water until no lumps remain. Add 1 tablespoon butter, salt, 1 cup sugar, and 1/2 teaspoon vanilla. Reduce heat; simmer while making batter. Preheat oven to 400°F. Combine flour and remaining 1/4 cup sugar in bowl. Melt remaining 1 tablespoon butter in saucepan; stir in milk and remaining 1/2 teaspoon vanilla until blended. Add to flour mixture; blend well. Drop by tablespoonfuls into hot syrup. Place skillet in oven. Bake 25 minutes. To serve, remove dumplings with slotted spoon. Turn upside down into dessert dishes. Spoon syrup over each. Top with sweetened whipped cream, if desired.

Dixie Cobbler _____ 6 to 8 servings

2 cups sifted Martha White
Self-Rising Flour
2/3 cup vegetable shortening
3 to 4 tablespoons cold water
1 1/4 to 2 cups sugar
2 tablespoons cornstarch
4 cups fresh or frozen
sliced peaches or
blackberries

1/2 teaspoon almond extract,
or 1 teaspoon lemon
juice
1/2 cup butter or margarine
2 tablespoons sugar

Place flour in bowl. Cut in half of the shortening with pastry blender or 2 knives until mixture is consistency of coarse crumbs. Cut in remaining shortening until mixture is consistency of small peas. Sprinkle water, 1 tablespoon at a time, over mixture; stir with fork until mixture leaves sides of bowl. Shape into ball. Wrap in waxed paper; set aside. Preheat oven to 375°F. Combine 1 1/4 to 2 cups sugar (according to tartness of fruit) and cornstarch in small bowl; blend well. Add fruit and flavoring (almond extract for peaches or lemon juice for blackberries); toss lightly to mix; set aside. Divide dough into thirds. Gather 2 thirds into ball. Roll out into circle to fit bottom and sides of 2-quart casserole; line casserole with dough. Arrange fruit mixture over dough in casserole. Dot with butter, reserving 2 tablespoons for top. Roll out remaining dough into circle 1/2 inch larger than top of casserole. Cover filling with pastry circle, pressing edge down side of casserole. Dot with remaining 2 tablespoons butter. Sprinkle with 2 tablespoons sugar. Bake 55 minutes, or until golden brown.

Cobbler may bubble over toward end of baking time. For easy cleanup, place a pan or piece of aluminum foil under casserole in oven.

From One Neighbor To Another

Across the fence or down the street, your friendship will take on a very special meaning when you share our Smoky Mountain Jam Cake, Old South Sweet Potato Pie, or Teatime Tassies with friends and neighbors. Any time you want to share good baking with good friends, start looking here for the perfect gift. Remember, large or small, the best gifts come in sweet packages.

Derby Day Rolls _____ 36 rolls

2 cups water
1 cup vegetable shortening
6 1/2 to 7 cups sifted Martha White
　All-Purpose Flour,
　divided
1 1/2 cups sugar, divided
1 teaspoon salt

1 package (1/4 ounce) active
　dry yeast
2 eggs, room temperature
4 teaspoons cinnamon
1/4 cup butter or margarine,
　melted
Rum Icing (below)

Grease large bowl; set aside. Heat water and shortening in saucepan until very warm (120°F to 130°F). Combine 3 cups flour, 1 cup sugar, salt, and yeast in mixing bowl. Add heated mixture and eggs; beat with electric mixer until smooth. Add 2 cups flour; blend well. Stir in enough remaining flour to make a soft dough. Turn out onto lightly floured board or pastry cloth. Cover and let rest 10 minutes. Knead 8 to 10 minutes, or until smooth and elastic. Shape into ball. Place in prepared bowl. Turn once to grease top. Cover and let rise in warm place, free from draft, 1 1/2 hours, or until double in bulk. Combine remaining 1/2 cup sugar and cinnamon in small dish; set aside. Grease 36 muffin cups; set aside. Punch dough down; divide in half. Roll out each half on lightly floured board or pastry cloth into 15 × 10-inch rectangle. Brush each with half of the butter. Sprinkle each with half of the sugar-cinnamon mixture. Roll up, jelly-roll fashion, from long side. Cut into 3/4-inch thick slices. Place slices, cut sides down, in prepared muffin cups. Cover and let rise in warm place, free from draft, 30 minutes, or until double in bulk. Preheat oven to 400°F. Bake 20 minutes. Transfer to wire racks to cool. Drizzle tops with Rum Icing.

Rum Icing

1 1/2 cups confectioners sugar
1/4 cup milk

1 teaspoon rum extract

Combine all ingredients in small mixing bowl; beat with electric mixer until smooth.

If you do not have 36 muffin cups, you can bake 12 rolls, cut sides down, in greased 8-inch round baking pan. Sides of rolls will be soft.

Smoky Mountain Jam Cake _____ 1 cake

1 cup sugar	1/2 teaspoon allspice
3/4 cup butter or margarine	1/4 teaspoon baking soda
1/2 teaspoon vanilla	1/4 cup buttermilk
3 eggs	1/2 cup strawberry preserves
1 1/2 cups sifted Martha White	1/2 cup fresh or frozen
Self-Rising Flour	blackberries, drained
1/2 teaspoon cinnamon	1 cup plum jelly
1/2 teaspoon ground cloves	Caramel Icing (page 107)

Preheat oven to 325°F. Grease and flour two 8-inch square or 9-inch round baking pans; set aside. Cream sugar and butter with electric mixer in mixing bowl until light and fluffy. Add vanilla; blend well. Add eggs, 1 at a time, beating well after each addition. Sift flour, cinnamon, cloves, allspice, and baking soda into separate bowl; repeat sifting. Alternately beat flour mixture and buttermilk into creamed mixture, beginning and ending with flour mixture. Stir in preserves and blackberries; blend well. Pour into prepared pans. Bake 45 to 50 minutes, or until toothpick inserted in centers comes out clean. Cool in pans on wire racks. Turn out of pans. Place bottom layer on cake plate. Spread plum jelly evenly over layer. Add top layer. Wrap in aluminum foil. Store at room temperature 1 to 2 days to develop flavor. Frost wtih Caramel Icing.

Fried Fruit Pies _____ 6 pies

1 cup cooked dried fruit	1/2 teaspoon nutmeg
(such as apricots,	1/2 teaspoon cinnamon
peaches, apples, pears,	Pastry for 1-crust pie;
prunes, or raisins),	use 1/4 cup vegetable
drained	shortening (page 76)
1 teaspoon lemon juice	Oil for deep-fat frying
1/2 cup sugar	

Combine fruit, lemon juice, sugar, nutmeg, and cinnamon in small bowl; set aside. Roll out pastry on floured board or pastry cloth to 1/4-inch thickness. Use sharp knife to cut into six 5 1/2-inch rounds. (Use saucer as guide for size.) Place 2 to 3 tablespoons fruit mixture on 1 half of each round. Fold pastry in half over filling; pinch edges to seal. Refrigerate 1 hour. Preheat oil in deep fryer or large skillet to 375°F. Cook 8 to 10 minutes, turning to brown evenly.

Carolina Coffeecake ———— 1 coffeecake

1/2 cup firmly packed brown
    sugar
2 tablespoons Martha White
    All-Purpose Flour
1 teaspoon cinnamon
2 tablespoons butter or
    margarine

3/4 cup sugar
1/3 cup vegetable shortening
2 eggs
1 3/4 cups sifted Martha White
    Self-Rising Flour
3/4 cup milk
1/3 cup chopped nuts

Preheat oven to 375°F. Grease 10-inch round baking pan or iron skillet; set aside. Combine brown sugar, all-purpose flour, cinnamon, and butter in small bowl; blend with pastry blender or 2 knives until mixture is consistency of coarse crumbs; set aside. Cream sugar and shortening with electric mixer in mixing bowl until light and fluffy. Add eggs, 1 at a time, beating well after each addition. Alternately beat in self-rising flour and milk, in thirds. Stir in nuts. Pour into prepared pan. Sprinkle with brown sugar mixture. Bake 30 to 35 minutes, or until toothpick inserted in center comes out clean.

If using Martha White All-Purpose Flour, sift 2 1/2 teaspoons baking powder and 1/2 teaspoon salt with flour.

Granny's Tea Cakes ———— 28 cookies

3/4 cup sugar
1/2 cup butter or margarine
1/2 teaspoon salt
1 teaspoon vanilla
1/2 teaspoon lemon or orange
    extract

2 eggs
2 cups Martha White
    All-Purpose Flour
1 teaspoon baking powder

Cream sugar, butter, salt, vanilla, and lemon extract with electric mixer in mixing bowl until light and fluffy. Add eggs, 1 at a time, beating well after each addition. Combine flour and baking powder in separate bowl. Add flour mixture to creamed mixture; blend well. Refrigerate at least 1 hour. Preheat oven to 400°F. Divide dough in half. Roll out each half on lightly floured board or pastry cloth to 1/4-inch thickness. Cut out with floured 3-inch cookie cutter. Place on ungreased baking sheets. Bake 10 to 12 minutes, or until lightly browned. Transfer to wire racks to cool.

Richland Country Pie _____ 8 servings

2 eggs, at room temperature
1 cup sugar
1 cup Martha White
  All-Purpose Flour
1/2 cup butter or margarine,
  melted and cooled
1 teaspoon vanilla
1 cup chopped walnuts or
  pecans
1 package (6 ounces)
  semisweet chocolate
  pieces
1 unbaked 9-inch pie shell
  (page 76), chilled

Preheat oven to 375°F. Lightly beat eggs with electric mixer in mixing bowl. Add sugar, flour, butter, and vanilla; mix until smooth. Stir in nuts and chocolate. Pour into pie shell. Bake 35 to 40 minutes, or until knife inserted in center comes out clean. Cool in pan on wire rack.

Sea Island Bars _____ 16 bars

1/2 cup butter or margarine
1/2 cup sugar
1/3 cup firmly packed brown
  sugar
2 tablespoons water
1 cup sifted Martha White
  Self-Rising Flour
1 egg
1 teaspoon vanilla
1/2 cup chopped nuts
1/2 cup shredded coconut
1 package (6 ounces)
  semisweet chocolate
  pieces

Preheat oven to 350°F. Grease 9-inch square baking pan; set aside. Melt butter in 2-quart saucepan over very low heat. Remove from heat. Add sugars and water; blend well. Stir in flour. Add egg and vanilla; blend thoroughly. Add nuts, coconut, and chocolate; blend well. Pour into prepared pan. Bake 30 minutes. Cool in pan. Cut into bars.

Cheese Grits Casserole ____ 6 to 8 servings

4 cups water
1 teaspoon salt
1 cup Martha White Quick
  Grits
4 eggs, lightly beaten
1 1/4 cups (5 ounces) grated sharp
  Cheddar cheese, divided
1 cup milk
1/2 cup butter or margarine
Dash cayenne

Preheat oven to 350°F. Grease 2-quart casserole; set aside. Bring water and salt to boil in large saucepan. Slowly stir in grits; cook 4 to 5 minutes, stirring occasionally. Remove from heat. Stir small amount grits mixture into eggs. Return all to saucepan. Add 1 cup cheese, milk, butter, and cayenne; blend well. Pour into prepared casserole. Sprinkle with remaining 1/4 cup cheese. Bake 1 hour, or until cheese is golden brown.

Delta Pecan Pie _____ 1 pie

3 eggs, lightly beaten	1/4 teaspoon salt
1 cup sugar	1 teaspoon vanilla
1 cup dark corn syrup	1 cup pecans
2 tablespoons butter or margarine, melted	1 unbaked 9-inch pie shell (page 76), chilled

Preheat oven to 375°F. Combine eggs, sugar, corn syrup, butter, salt, and vanilla in bowl; blend until smooth. Stir in pecans. Pour into pie shell. Bake 40 to 45 minutes, or until filling is set. Cool in pan on wire rack.

Southern Sweet Potato Bread _____ 1 loaf

1/2 cup firmly packed brown sugar	1 teaspoon grated orange peel
1/4 cup butter or margarine	2 cups sifted Martha White Self-Rising Flour
2 eggs, lightly beaten	1/4 teaspoon nutmeg
1 cup mashed cooked sweet potatoes	1/4 teaspoon allspice
3 tablespoons milk	1/2 cup chopped nuts

Preheat oven to 350°F. Grease 9 × 5 × 3-inch loaf pan; set aside. Cream brown sugar and butter with electric mixer in mixing bowl until light and fluffy. Add eggs, sweet potatoes, milk, and orange peel; blend well. Add flour, nutmeg, and allspice; blend well. Stir in nuts. Pour into prepared pan. Bake 45 to 50 minutes, or until toothpick inserted in center comes out clean. Cool in pan 10 minutes. Gently loosen sides of loaf. Turn out onto wire rack to cool completely.

In 1953, Martha White hired an unknown country music group who toured the Southland as spokesmen for the company. That group, Lester Flatt, Earl Scruggs, and the Foggy Mountain Boys, later went on to become the nation's number one bluegrass music group.

Delta Pecan Pie →

Teatime Tassies ——————————— 24 muffins

1 package (3 ounces) cream cheese, at room temperature
1/2 cup plus 2 tablespoons butter or margarine, softened, divided
1 cup sifted Martha White All-Purpose Flour

1 1/2 cups firmly packed brown sugar
2 eggs
2 teaspoons vanilla
1/2 teaspoon salt
1 1/3 cups coarsely chopped pecans

Combine cream cheese and 1/2 cup butter in bowl; blend well. Stir in flour; blend well. Refrigerate about 1 hour. Preheat oven to 325°F. Cream brown sugar and remaining 2 tablespoons butter with electric mixer in small mixing bowl. Add eggs, vanilla, and salt; beat until smooth. Stir in pecans. Remove dough from refrigerator and divide into 24 pieces; roll into balls. Press balls into bottoms and up sides of ungreased miniature muffin cups. Spoon 1 heaping teaspoon pecan mixture into each cup. Bake 25 minutes, or until filling is set. Cool completely in pans.

Mississippi Mud Cake ——————————— 1 cake

2 cups sugar
1 cup vegetable shortening
4 eggs
1 1/2 cups sifted Martha White All-Purpose Flour
1/3 cup cocoa

1/2 teaspoon salt
2 teaspoons vanilla
1 cup chopped nuts
2 cups miniature marshmallows
Mississippi Mud Icing (page 133)

Preheat oven to 325°F. Grease and flour 13 × 9 × 2-inch baking pan; set aside. Cream sugar and shortening with electric mixer in mixing bowl until light and fluffy. Add eggs; beat at low speed until well blended. Combine flour, cocoa, and salt in separate bowl. Add to creamed mixture; blend well. Stir in vanilla and nuts. Pour into prepared pan. Bake 35 to 40 minutes, or until toothpick inserted in center comes out clean. Remove from oven. Sprinkle marshmallows evenly over top. Return to oven 10 minutes, or until marshmallows are melted. Cool in pan on wire rack. Frost with Mississippi Mud Icing. Chill before cutting into squares.

Mississippi Mud Icing

4 1/2 cups (16 ounces)
  confectioners sugar,
  sifted
1/3 cup cocoa
1 cup butter or margarine,
  melted

1/2 cup evaporated milk,
  undiluted, or
  half-and-half
1 teaspoon vanilla
1/2 cup chopped nuts

Combine confectioners sugar and cocoa in small mixing bowl. Add butter; blend well. Add milk and vanilla; beat with electric mixer until smooth. Stir in nuts.

Old Virginia Spoon Bread _____ 6 to 8 servings

1 1/2 cups boiling water
1 cup Martha White
  Self-Rising Corn Meal
3 eggs, separated

1 tablespoon butter or
  margarine
1 cup buttermilk
1 teaspoon sugar

Preheat oven to 375°F. Grease 2-quart baking dish; set aside. Pour water over corn meal in bowl; stir until slightly cooled. Beat egg yolks with electric mixer in mixing bowl until lemon-colored. Stir egg yolks and butter into corn meal; blend well. Stir in buttermilk and sugar. Beat egg whites in separate bowl until soft peaks form. Fold egg whites into corn meal mixture until blended. Pour into prepared baking dish. Bake 45 to 50 minutes. Serve hot with butter.

Miss Martha's Chess Pie _____ 1 pie

1 1/3 cups sugar
1/2 cup butter or margarine
1 tablespoon Martha White
  Self-Rising Corn Meal
1/3 cup half-and-half

1 teaspoon white vinegar
3 eggs
1 teaspoon vanilla
1 unbaked 9-inch pie shell
  (page 76), chilled

Preheat oven to 350°F. Cream sugar and butter with electric mixer in mixing bowl until light and fluffy. Add corn meal, half-and-half, and vinegar; blend well. Add eggs, 1 at a time, beating well after each addition. Add vanilla; blend well. Pour into pie shell. Bake 50 minutes, or until knife inserted about 1 inch from edge comes out clean. Center will set as it cools. Cool in pan on wire rack about 2 hours.

Lemon Rub Pie _____ 1 pie

1 3/4 cups sugar
  2 tablespoons Martha White
    Self-Rising Corn Meal
  1 tablespoon Martha White
    Self-Rising Flour
  4 eggs, lightly beaten
1/4 cup butter or margarine,
    melted

1/4 cup milk
1/4 cup lemon juice
  2 tablespoons grated lemon
    peel
  1 unbaked 9-inch pie shell
    (page 76)

Preheat oven to 375°F. Combine sugar, corn meal, and flour in bowl. Add eggs, butter, milk, lemon juice, and lemon peel; blend well. Pour into pie shell. Bake 35 to 40 minutes, or until browned. Cool in pan on wire rack.

Old South Sweet
Potato Pie _____ 1 pie

1 1/3 cups sugar
1/2 cup butter or margarine
  1 tablespoon Martha White
    Self-Rising Corn Meal
1/3 cup half-and-half
  3 eggs
  1 cup mashed cooked sweet
    potatoes

1/2 teaspoon nutmeg
1/2 teaspoon cinnamon
1/4 teaspoon salt
  1 teaspoon vanilla
  1 unbaked 9-inch pie shell
    (page 76), chilled

Preheat oven to 350°F. Cream sugar and butter with electric mixer in mixing bowl until light and fluffy. Add corn meal and half-and-half; blend well. Add eggs, 1 at a time, beating well after each addition. Add sweet potatoes, nutmeg, cinnamon, salt, and vanilla; blend well. Pour into pie shell. Bake 50 minutes, or until knife inserted 1 inch from edge comes out clean. Cool in pan on wire rack.

The Bake Sale

The annual bake sale boasts a wide array of tempting baked goods. It's great fun because you always know whose cakes, breads, and cookies are the very best to take home. Try any one of the recipes in this chapter, and bring the best of the bake sale into your own kitchen. Everyone will be delighted because it's been baked by the best — you.

Sugar Plum Pudding _____ 1 cake

2 cups sifted Martha White Self-Rising Flour	3 eggs
1 1/2 cups sugar	1 cup buttermilk
1 teaspoon nutmeg	1 teaspoon vanilla
1 teaspoon allspice	1 cup cooked finely chopped prunes
1 teaspoon cinnamon	1 cup chopped nuts
3/4 cup vegetable oil	Glaze (below)

Preheat oven to 325°F. Grease and flour one 15 × 10 × 2-inch or two 8-inch square baking pans; set aside. Sift flour, sugar, nutmeg, allspice, and cinnamon into large bowl. Add remaining ingredients, except Glaze, mixing well after each addition. Pour into prepared pan. Bake 40 to 45 minutes, or until toothpick inserted in center comes out clean. While cake is baking, prepare Glaze. Remove cake from oven. Pour Glaze over cake in pan while hot. Serve from pan. Cake will keep 3 to 4 days stored in refrigerator.

Glaze

1 cup sugar	1 tablespoon white corn syrup
1/2 cup buttermilk	1 teaspoon vanilla
1/2 cup butter or margarine	

Combine all ingredients in saucepan. Bring to a boil, stirring constantly. Remove from heat.

This is a traditional version of Martha White Prune Cake.

Gingersnaps _____ About 60 cookies

1 cup firmly packed dark brown sugar	1 teaspoon baking soda
3/4 cup vegetable shortening	1 teaspoon ginger
1/4 cup molasses	1 teaspoon cinnamon
1 egg	1/2 teaspoon ground cloves
2 1/4 cups sifted Martha White Self-Rising Flour	1/4 cup sugar

Preheat oven to 375°F. Grease 2 large baking sheets; set aside. Cream brown sugar and shortening with electric mixer in mixing bowl until light and fluffy. Add molasses and egg; blend thoroughly. Sift in flour, baking soda, and spices; blend thoroughly. Shape dough into 3/4-inch balls. Roll in sugar to coat. Place about 2 inches apart on prepared baking sheets. Bake 10 minutes, or until tops are crinkly.

Old-Fashioned Oatmeal Cookies _____ About 36 cookies

1/2 cup raisins
Boiling water
1 cup sifted Martha White
  Self-Rising Flour
3/4 teaspoon cinnamon
1/4 teaspoon nutmeg
1/4 teaspoon baking soda

1/4 cup sugar
1/2 cup firmly packed brown
  sugar
1/3 cup vegetable shortening
1 egg
2 tablespoons milk
1 1/2 cups uncooked quick oats

Combine raisins and water in small bowl; set aside. Preheat oven to 375°F. Grease 2 large baking sheets; set aside. Sift flour, cinnamon, nutmeg, and baking soda into mixing bowl. Add sugars, shortening, egg, and milk; beat with electric mixer 2 minutes, or until smooth. Drain raisins; add oats and raisins to batter; blend well. Refrigerate about 20 minutes. Roll out dough on lightly floured board or pastry cloth to 1/4-inch thickness. Cut out with floured 2-inch cookie cutter. Place on prepared baking sheets. Bake 12 to 15 minutes, or until golden brown. Transfer immediately to wire racks to cool.

Pastry Pinwheels _____ 30 to 36 pinwheels

1 package (3 ounces) cream
  cheese, at room
  temperature
3/4 cup butter, softened,
  divided
1 egg yolk

1 cup sifted Martha White
  All-Purpose Flour
1/2 cup finely chopped nuts
1/3 cup sugar
2 teaspoons cinnamon
Confectioners sugar

Combine cream cheese and 1/2 cup butter in bowl; blend well. Add egg yolk and flour; blend well. Cover; refrigerate about 30 minutes. Preheat oven to 350°F. Divide dough in half. Roll out 1 half on lightly floured board or pastry cloth into 1/4-inch thick rectangle. Melt remaining 1/4 cup butter. Brush half of the melted butter over rectangle. Combine nuts, sugar, and cinnamon in small bowl. Sprinkle half of the nut mixture over rectangle. Roll up, jelly-roll fashion, from long side. Cut into 1/2-inch thick slices. Place slices, cut sides down, on ungreased baking sheet. Repeat with remaining dough. Bake 15 minutes, or until golden brown. Transfer to wire racks to cool. Sprinkle with confectioners sugar.

County Fair Bread _____ 1 loaf

6 to 6 1/2 cups sifted Martha White All-Purpose Flour, divided	1 1/2 cups milk
1/4 cup sugar	1/4 cup butter or margarine
2 teaspoons salt	2 eggs, at room temperature
1 package (1/4 ounce) active dry yeast	1 egg white
	1 tablespoon water
	Sesame seed

Grease large bowl; set aside. Combine 1 cup flour, sugar, salt, and yeast in mixing bowl; set aside. Heat milk and butter in saucepan until very warm (120°F to 130°F); butter need not melt completely. Add heated mixture and eggs to flour mixture; blend well. Add 2 cups flour; beat with electric mixer 2 minutes. Stir in enough remaining flour to make a stiff dough. Turn out onto floured board or pastry cloth. Knead 8 to 10 minutes, or until smooth and elastic. Place in prepared bowl. Turn once to grease top. Cover and let rise in warm place, free from draft, 1 1/2 hours, or until double in bulk. Grease large baking sheet; set aside. Punch dough down. Turn out onto floured surface. Pinch off about one-third of dough; set aside. Divide remaining dough into thirds. Roll out each third into 18-inch rope. Braid ropes; pinch ends to seal. Place on prepared baking sheet. Divide remaining dough into thirds. Roll out each third into 12-inch rope. Braid ropes; pinch ends to seal. Place on top of large braid. Cover and let rise in warm place, free from draft, 1 hour, or until double in bulk. Preheat oven to 375°F. Beat egg white and water with fork in small dish. Brush braids with egg wash. Sprinkle with sesame seed. Bake 40 to 45 minutes, or until golden brown and loaf sounds hollow when lightly tapped. If bread begins to brown too rapidly, cover with tent of aluminum foil or brown paper.

Two single braids can be made by dividing dough in half. Bake 35 to 40 minutes.

County Fair Bread →

Date-Nut Loaf _____ 1 loaf

1 cup sugar	1 cup sifted Martha White
1/4 cup vegetable shortening	Self-Rising Flour
1 teaspoon vanilla	4 cups pecans, coarsely chopped
4 eggs	1 pound dates, chopped

Preheat oven to 300°F. Grease and flour 9 × 5 × 3-inch loaf pan; set aside. Cream sugar, shortening, and vanilla with electric mixer in mixing bowl until light and fluffy. Add eggs, 1 at a time, beating well after each addition. Gradually beat in flour; blend well. Add pecans and dates; blend well. Pour into prepared pan. Bake 1 1/2 hours. Cool completely in pan. Gently loosen sides of loaf before turning out of pan.

Applesauce Cake with
Hot Milk Icing _____ 1 cake

1 3/4 cups sugar	1/2 teaspoon nutmeg
1/4 cup firmly packed light	1/4 teaspoon allspice
brown sugar	1/4 teaspoon baking soda
1/2 cup butter or margarine	1 2/3 cups (16 1/2 ounces)
2 eggs	applesauce
2 1/2 cups sifted Martha White	2/3 cup raisins (optional)
Self-Rising Flour	1/4 cup chopped walnuts
1 teaspoon cinnamon	Hot Milk Icing (below)

Preheat oven to 350°F. Grease and flour 13 × 9 × 2-inch baking pan; set aside. Cream sugars and butter with electirc mixer in mixing bowl until light and fluffy. Add eggs, 1 at a time, beating well after each addition. Sift flour, cinnamon, nutmeg, allspice and baking soda into separate bowl. Alternately add flour mixture and applesauce to creamed mixture; blend well. Stir in raisins and nuts. Pour into prepared pan. Bake 50 minutes, or until toothpick inserted in center comes out clean. Spread Hot Milk Icing over warm cake. Cool completely in pan.

Hot Milk Icing

2 cups confectioners sugar,	2 tablespoons butter, melted
sifted	1/2 teaspoon vanilla or rum
1/4 cup hot milk	flavoring

Combine all ingredients in small mixing bowl; beat with electric mixer until smooth.

Chocolate Chip Cookies _____ About 30 cookies

1/2 cup sugar	1 1/4 cups sifted Martha White
1/3 cup firmly packed brown	Self-Rising Flour
sugar	1 package (6 ounces) semisweet
1/2 cup butter or margarine	chocolate pieces
1 egg	1/2 cup chopped nuts
1 teaspoon vanilla	(optional)

Preheat oven to 375°F. Lightly grease 2 large baking sheets; set aside. Cream sugars and butter with electric mixer in mixing bowl until light and fluffy. Add egg and vanilla; blend well. Add flour; blend well. Stir in chocolate and nuts. Drop by teaspoonfuls 2 inches apart onto prepared baking sheets. Bake 10 to 12 minutes, or until golden brown. Transfer to wire racks to cool.

Cinnamon Raisin Bread _____ 2 loaves

1 recipe Sweet Yeast Dough	1 cup sugar
(page 55)	2 tablespoons cinnamon
1/2 cup raisins	
1/4 cup butter or margarine,	
melted	

Prepare Sweet Yeast Dough. After dough has risen, punch down; let rest 10 minutes. Grease two 9 × 5 × 3-inch loaf pans; set aside. Lightly knead raisins into dough. Divide dough in half. Roll out each half into 9 × 7-inch rectangle. Brush each rectangle with half of the butter. Combine sugar and cinnamon in small bowl; blend well. Sprinkle each rectangle with half of the sugar-cinnamon mixture. Roll up, jelly-roll fashion, from long side. Fold ends under; press edges to seal. Place in prepared pans. Cover and let rise in warm place, free from draft, 45 minutes, or until double in bulk. Preheat oven to 375°F. Bake 30 to 35 minutes, or until loaves sound hollow when lightly tapped. Turn out onto wire racks to cool. Frost with Confectioners Icing (page 44), if desired.

Cranberry Banana Nut Bread _____ 1 cake

1 1/2 cups sugar
2/3 cup vegetable shortening
3 eggs
3 1/2 cups sifted Martha White
    Self-Rising Flour
1 cup chopped walnuts

1/4 teaspoon baking soda
2 cups mashed bananas
    (4 medium)
1 can (16 ounces) whole
    berry cranberry sauce

Preheat oven to 325°F. Grease and flour 12-cup bundt-type pan; set aside. Cream sugar and shortening with electric mixer in mixing bowl until light and fluffy. Add eggs; blend well. Add flour, walnuts, baking soda, and bananas; blend well. Stir in cranberry sauce. Pour into prepared pan. Bake 1 hour 10 minutes to 1 hour 15 minutes, or until toothpick inserted in center comes out clean. Cool in pan 10 minutes. Turn out onto wire rack to cool.

If using Martha White All-Purpose Flour, add 4 teaspoons baking powder, 3/4 teaspoon salt, and increase baking soda to 1/2 teaspoon.

Chocolate Pound Cake _____ 1 cake

3 cups sifted Martha White
    All-Purpose Flour
1/2 cup cocoa
1/2 teaspoon salt
1/2 teaspoon baking powder
3 cups sugar

1 cup butter or margarine
1/2 cup vegetable shortening
5 eggs
1 cup milk
1 1/2 teaspoons vanilla

Preheat oven to 325°F. Grease 10-inch tube pan; set aside. Sift flour, cocoa, salt, and baking powder into large bowl; set aside. Cream sugar, butter, and shortening with electric mixer in mixing bowl until light and fluffy. Add eggs, 1 at a time, beating well after each addition. Alternately beat in flour mixture and milk, beginning and ending with flour mixture. Stir in vanilla. Pour into prepared pan. Bake 1 1/2 hours, or until toothpick inserted in center comes out clean. Cool in pan 10 minutes. Turn out onto wire rack to cool completely.

← Cranberry Banana Nut Bread

Dutch Apple Cake ——————— 2 coffeecakes

1/2 cup milk
1/4 cup vegetable shortening
2 1/2 to 3 cups sifted Martha White
    All-Purpose Flour,
    divided
3/4 cup sugar
1 package (1/4 ounce) active
    dry yeast

1 egg
2 to 3 large apples, peeled
    and thinly sliced
1/2 teaspoon cinnamon
2 tablespoons butter or
    margarine

Grease large bowl; set aside. Heat milk and shortening in saucepan until very warm (120°F to 130°F); set aside. Combine 1 cup flour, 1/4 cup sugar, and yeast in large mixing bowl. Beat at low speed of electric mixer just until moistened, gradually adding milk mixture. Scrape bowl with rubber spatula; beat at medium speed 2 minutes. Add egg and 1 cup flour; beat 2 minutes. Stir in enough remaining flour to make a soft dough. Turn out onto lightly floured board or pastry cloth. Knead 8 to 10 minutes, or until smooth and elastic. Place in prepared bowl. Turn once to grease top. Cover and let rise in warm place, free from draft, 1 hour, or until double in bulk. Grease two 9-inch round baking pans; set aside. Punch dough down; divide in half. Pat 1 half into each prepared pan, forming a ridge halfway up side of pan. Arrange half of the apples in pinwheel pattern over dough in each pan. Combine remaining 1/2 cup sugar and cinnamon in small dish; blend well. Set aside 2 tablespoons sugar-cinnamon mixture. Sprinkle half of the remaining sugar-cinnamon mixture over apples. Dot each with half of the butter. Cover and let rise in warm place, free from draft, 25 minutes, or until double in bulk. Preheat oven to 400°F. Cover pans with aluminum foil. Bake 10 minutes. Remove foil; bake 25 to 30 minutes, or until golden brown. Transfer, apple side up, to wire racks to cool. Sprinkle with reserved sugar-cinnamon mixture. Serve warm.

Alice Jarman, past test kitchen director, likes to tell about the time she was watching some little 4-H members do their baking demonstrations. The judges were asking questions, and one little girl said she was going to put her dough "in a warm place to rise." The judge asked "How warm?" She couldn't answer, but a friend came to her rescue and said, "Well, I don't know, but my mother says if it's too hot to sit there, it's too hot for the dough." That is still a pretty good test!

Mexican Sweet Bread ———— About 32 buns

1 recipe Sweet Yeast Dough (page 55)	1 cup butter or margarine, melted
2 cups sugar	2 eggs, lightly beaten
2 cups sifted Martha White All-Purpose Flour	1 teaspoon cinnamon
	Dash salt

Prepare Sweet Yeast Dough. After dough has risen, punch down; let rest 10 minutes. Grease 2 large baking sheets; set aside. Combine remaining ingredients in bowl; blend well; set aside. Shape pieces of dough into smooth 1 3/4-inch balls. Flatten balls with palm of hand or rolling pin into 4-inch rounds. Place rounds about 2 inches apart on prepared baking sheets. Place heaping tablespoonful of sugar mixture on center of each round; spread almost to edges. Cover and let rise in warm place, free from draft, 30 minutes, or until double in bulk. Preheat oven to 400°F. Bake 10 minutes, or until lightly browned. Cool 3 to 4 minutes on wire rack before serving.

Sour Cream Pound Cake ———— 1 cake

3 cups sifted Martha White All-Purpose Flour	6 eggs
1/4 teaspoon salt	2 teaspoons vanilla
1/4 teaspoon baking soda	1/2 teaspoon almond extract
3 cups sugar	1 cup (8 ounces) dairy sour cream
1 cup butter or margarine	

Preheat oven to 325°F. Grease and flour 10-inch tube or 12-cup bundt-type pan; set aside. Combine flour, salt, and baking soda in large bowl; set aside. Cream sugar and butter with electric mixer in mixing bowl until fluffy. Add eggs, 1 at a time, beating well after each addition. Beat in vanilla and almond extract. Alternately beat in flour mixture and sour cream, beginning and ending with flour. Pour into prepared pan. Bake 1 hour 15 minutes, or until toothpick inserted in center comes out clean. Cool 30 minutes in pan. Turn out onto wire rack to cool completely.

Tawny Almond Fruitcake _____ 1 cake

2 cups slivered blanched almonds	3 1/4 cups sifted Martha White All-Purpose Flour, divided
1 1/2 cups candied cherries, halved	1 1/2 cups sugar
3/4 cup seedless golden raisins	1 cup butter or margarine
1/2 cup diced candied pineapple	4 eggs
1/2 cup dried apricot halves, chopped	1 1/2 teaspoons almond extract
	1 1/2 teaspoons baking powder
	1/4 teaspoon salt
	3 tablespoons orange juice

Preheat oven to 250°F. Generously grease and flour 10-inch tube or 12-cup bundt-type pan; set aside. Spread almonds in shallow baking pan; bake in oven 20 minutes, stirring occasionally, until golden brown; set aside. Combine cherries, raisins, pineapple, apricots, and 1/4 cup flour in small bowl; toss lightly to mix; set aside. Cream sugar and butter with electric mixer in mixing bowl until fluffy. Add eggs, 1 at a time, beating well after each addition. Add almond extract; blend well; set aside. Sift remaining 3 cups flour, baking powder, and salt into large bowl. Alternately add flour mixture and orange juice to creamed mixture, beginning and ending with flour mixture; blend well. Stir in toasted almonds and fruit mixture. Pour into prepared pan. Bake 3 to 3 1/2 hours. Cool completely in pan. Wrap in aluminum foil or plastic wrap. Store in refrigerator.

In the summer of 1963, Martha White introduced the pre-measured baking pouch, which offered a new convenience to the cook. The first product was BixMix which sold for ten cents. Its slogan, "Only a dime . . . And a squirt of water . . . Make you the world's best biscuit maker with Martha White's BixMix. Goodness gracious, it's good!" created a sensation in packaging that caused the on-hand supplies to become depleted in six short days.

As Quick As 1-2-3

Thanks to the wonderful convenience packages available today, your pantry holds the key to many last-minute treats. Whether it's unexpected company, an "I forgot" dessert, or a late-night snack, you'll find these recipes tailored to your spur-of-the-moment needs.

BixMix Brownies _____ 36 bars

1/2 cup butter or margarine	1 package (5 1/2 ounces)
1 1/2 squares (1 1/2 ounces)	Martha White BixMix
unsweetened chocolate	(1 1/3 cups)
1 cup sugar	1 teaspoon vanilla
1 egg	1/2 cup chopped nuts (optional)

Preheat oven to 350°F. Grease and lightly flour 8-inch square baking pan; set aside. Melt butter and chocolate in 2-quart saucepan over low heat. Add remaining ingredients; stir just until blended; beat four strokes. Pour into prepared pan. Bake 25 minutes. Brownies will be very moist. Transfer to wire racks to cool.

Brownies can be baked in greased and floured 9-inch pie pan. Cut into wedges while warm. Top with vanilla or peppermint ice cream.

BixMix Banana Loaf _____ 1 loaf

1 egg	2 packages (5 1/2 ounces each)
1 cup (2 or 3 medium) mashed	Martha White BixMix
ripe bananas	(2 2/3 cups)
1/4 cup buttermilk	1/4 teaspoon baking soda
2/3 cup sugar	1/2 cup chopped nuts

Preheat oven to 350°F. Grease and lightly flour bottom of 9 × 5 × 3-inch loaf pan; set aside. Beat egg in bowl with fork. Stir in bananas and buttermilk. Add sugar, baking mix, and baking soda; stir until smooth. Stir in nuts. Pour into prepared pan. Bake 50 to 55 minutes, or until toothpick inserted in center comes out clean. Cool completely in pan on wire rack. Loaf slices better if wrapped and stored 1 day before serving.

Hobo Hoe Cakes _____ 8 servings

1 package (6 ounces)	3/4 cups water
Martha White "Cotton	Vegetable shortening or
Pickin' Cornbread" Mix	bacon drippings

Combine cornbread mix and water in bowl. Mix until well blended. Melt shortening 1/8 inch deep in large hot skillet. Pour batter, 1/4 cup at a time, into skillet. Cook cakes, turning once, until golden brown on both sides. Serve hot with butter.

Quick Cheese Quiche ——————— 1 quiche

2 tablespoons butter or
  margarine
1 small onion, chopped
4 strips bacon, crisp-cooked
  and crumbled
3 eggs, lightly beaten
1 cup (4 ounces) grated
  sharp Cheddar cheese

1/2 cup Martha White BixMix
1 1/2 cups milk
1/4 teaspoon salt
1/2 teaspoon dry mustard
  Dash cayenne
1 can (3 1/2 ounces) sliced
  mushrooms, drained
  (optional)

Preheat oven to 375°F. Butter 10-inch quiche, pie, or 9-inch square baking pan; set aside. Melt butter in small saucepan. Sauté onion in butter until transparent. Combine onion, bacon, eggs, cheese, baking mix, milk, and seasonings in bowl; mix thoroughly. Stir in mushrooms. Pour into prepared pan. Bake 35 minutes, or until knife inserted in center comes out clean. Let stand 5 minutes. Cut into wedges or squares.

Praline Muffins ——————— 12 muffins

6 tablespoons butter or
  margarine, melted
1/2 cup firmly packed brown
  sugar
6 teaspoons water
36 pecan halves

1 cup (8 ounces) dairy
  sour cream
1/4 cup milk
1 1/2 cups Martha White
  BixMix

Preheat oven to 425°F. Spoon 1 1/2 teaspoons butter, 2 teaspoons brown sugar, and 1/2 teaspoon water into each of 12 ungreased muffin cups. Arrange 3 pecan halves on top of brown sugar mixture in each cup. Combine sour cream, milk, and baking mix in bowl; stir until well blended. Spoon dough evenly into muffin cups. Bake 12 to 15 minutes, or until golden brown. Immediately invert pan onto serving plate. Let stand until syrup drizzles over sides of muffins.

To make Praline Coffeecake, combine butter, brown sugar, water, and pecan halves in bottom of 9-inch square baking pan. Combine sour cream, milk, and baking mix in bowl; stir until well blended. Spoon evenly over brown sugar mixture. Bake at 425°F 15 to 20 minutes, or until golden brown. Immediately turn out onto serving plate.

Strawberry Yogurt Muffins _____ 8 muffins

1/2 cup (4 ounces) strawberry
    yogurt
1 package (7 ounces)
    Martha White Strawberry
    Muffin Mix

1/4 cup water

Preheat oven to 425°F. Grease 8 muffin cups; set aside. Stir yogurt to blend fruit. Combine muffin mix, yogurt, and water in bowl; stir just to moisten. Fill prepared muffin cups two-thirds full. Bake 15 minutes, or until golden brown.

Apricot Bran Muffins _____ 8 muffins

1 egg
1/3 cup milk
1 tablespoon brown sugar
1/2 teaspoon cinnamon

1 package (7 ounces)
    Martha White Bran
    Muffin Mix
1/3 cup chopped dried apricots

Preheat oven to 425°F. Grease 8 muffin cups; set aside. Beat egg in bowl with fork. Add milk, brown sugar, and cinnamon; stir until sugar is dissolved. Add muffin mix and apricots; stir just until blended; batter will be lumpy. Fill prepared muffin cups two-thirds full. Bake 15 to 18 minutes, or until golden brown. Serve warm.

Homemade Crackers _____ 70 crackers

1 package (6 1/2 ounces)
    Martha White Pizza
    Crust Mix

Coarse salt

Preheat oven to 375°F. Grease 2 large baking sheets; set aside. Prepare pizza dough according to package directions. After dough rests 5 minutes, divide in half. Use rolling pin to roll out each half on lightly floured board or pastry cloth into 14 × 10-inch rectangle. (Dough must be very thin to make crisp crackers.) Ease rolled dough onto prepared baking sheets. Use sharp knife to score into squares. Sprinkle with coarse salt. Bake 12 to 15 minutes. Watch closely; crackers will brown quickly.

← Strawberry Yogurt Muffins, Apricot Bran Muffins, Praline Muffins (page 149)

Crêpes _____ 15 to 18 crêpes

1 egg	1 tablespoon butter or
1 1/2 cups milk	margarine, divided
1 package (5 1/2 ounces)	
Martha White FlapStax	

Combine egg and milk in mixing bowl; mix lightly with fork. Add pancake mix; beat with electric mixer until smooth. Melt 1/2 teaspoon butter in crêpe pan or small skillet. Spread over surface of hot pan. (A pastry brush works well for this.) Slowly pour in about 2 tablespoons batter, tipping pan to coat bottom. Cook over moderate heat until bottom is browned. Carefully turn crêpe with spatula or loosen edge and turn by hand. Brown other side. Butter pan as necessary between crêpes.

BixMix Doughnut Puffs _____ 20 puffs

Oil for deep-fat frying	1 package (5 1/2 ounces)
3/4 cup plus 2 tablespoons	Martha White BixMix
sugar, divided	1 egg, lightly beaten
2 tablespoons cinnamon	1/4 cup water

Preheat oil in deep-fat fryer to 350°F, or heat 1 1/4 inches oil in large skillet. Combine 3/4 cup sugar and cinnamon in paper bag; set aside. Combine baking mix, egg, water, and remaining 2 tablespoons sugar in bowl; beat just until smooth. Drop batter by teaspoonfuls into hot oil. Deep fry until golden brown, turning to brown evenly. Remove puffs with slotted spoon. Drop into bag containing sugar and cinnamon. Shake to coat puffs. Serve warm.

Coco Not Cookies _____ 48 cookies

1 cup sugar	1 package (5 1/2 ounces)
1/3 cup butter or margarine	Martha White BixMix
1 teaspoon coconut extract	1 package (2 ounces)
1 egg	Martha White SpudFlakes

Preheat oven to 375°F. Cream sugar, butter and coconut extract with electric mixer in mixing bowl. Add egg; blend well. Stir in baking mix and potato flakes; blend well. Shape dough into 3/4-inch balls. Place 2 inches apart on ungreased baking sheets. Bake 12 to 14 minutes, or until golden brown. Transfer to wire racks to cool.

Dough can be wrapped and frozen for later baking.

20 Penny Waffles —— Twelve 4 1/2-inch waffles

1 package (7 1/2 ounces)
    Martha White Corn
    Muffin Mix
1 package (5 1/2 ounces)
    Martha White FlapStax

1 3/4 cups water
1/3 cup butter or margarine,
    melted

Preheat waffle iron according to manufacturer's directions. Combine all ingredients in bowl; beat until smooth. Bake in hot waffle iron. If batter becomes too thick, add a little additional water. Serve with butter and syrup.

BixMix Riz Biscuits —————— 12 biscuits

1 1/3 teaspoons active dry yeast
1/3 cup warm water
    (110°F to 115°F)
1 tablespoon sugar

1 package (5 1/2 ounces) .
    Martha White BixMix
2 tablespoons butter, melted

Dissolve yeast in warm water in small bowl; set aside. Grease large baking sheet; set aside. Combine baking mix and sugar in bowl. Stir in yeast mixture. Turn out onto lightly floured board or pastry cloth. Knead 10 times, or until smooth. Roll out to 1/4-inch thickness. Cut into rounds with floured 2-inch biscuit cutter. Brush tops of rounds with butter. Stack 1 round on top of another to make a double biscuit. Repeat with remaining rounds. Place on prepared baking sheet. Cover and let rise in warm place, free from draft, 40 minutes, or until double in bulk. Preheat oven to 375°F. Bake 12 to 15 minutes, or until golden brown.

Crusty Dogs ————————————— 8 servings

1 package (6 1/2 ounces)
    Martha White Pizza
    Crust Mix

Prepared mustard
8 frankfurters

Preheat oven to 425°F. Lightly grease large baking sheet; set aside. Prepare pizza dough according to package directions. Cover and let rest 5 minutes. Turn out onto lightly floured board or pastry cloth. Knead 3 or 4 times, or until smooth. Roll out dough into 13-inch circle. Spread with mustard. Cut into 8 wedges. Place frankfurters on wide edge of each wedge. Roll up from wide end; pinch point into dough. Place on prepared baking sheet. Bake 15 to 17 minutes, or until golden brown. Serve hot.

Dessert Fruit Pizza _____ 12 to 16 servings

1 package (6 1/2 ounces)
   Martha White Pizza
   Crust Mix
2 tablespoons sugar
1 package (8 ounces) cream
   cheese, at room
   temperature
1 can (29 ounces) sliced
   peaches, drained;
   reserve syrup
1 can (4 ounces) sliced
   pineapple, drained;
   reserve syrup

1 firm banana, peeled and
   cut into 1/4-inch thick
   slices
12 hulled strawberries,
   cut in half
1/2 cup seedless green grapes
1 jar (10 ounces) apple
   jelly

Preheat oven to 425°F. Lightly grease 12-inch pizza pan; set aside. Prepare pizza dough according to package directions, adding sugar along with 1/2 cup water called for on package. Roll out dough on lightly floured board or pastry cloth into 12-inch circle. Place on prepared pan. Bake 15 to 20 minutes, or until golden brown. Cool in pan on wire rack. Combine cream cheese and 2 tablespoons peach syrup in mixing bowl; beat with electric mixer until smooth. Spread evenly over crust. Combine pineapple syrup and remaining peach syrup in bowl. Add bananas; set aside. Cut pineapple slices in half; set aside. Arrange strawberries in circle in center of crust. Arrange ring of grapes around strawberries. Drain bananas. Arrange pineapple, banana, and peach slices in rows to outside edge. Finish with strawberries and grapes. Melt jelly in small saucepan over low heat, stirring frequently, until smooth. Remove from heat; let stand until slightly thickened. Spoon evenly over fruit; use pastry brush to spread glaze evenly. Refrigerate until serving time. Cut into wedges or squares.

Other fruit can be used, such as kiwi, apricot halves, blueberries, raspberries, orange segments, apple slices, and pear slices. The syrup of canned fruit will help retard discoloring of fresh fruit.

Dessert Fruit Pizza →

INDEX

The Martha White Southern Baking Book